Cool Restaurants
Barcelona

teNeues

Imprint

Editor: Aurora Cuito

Photography: Roger Casas

Introduction: Aurora Cuito

Copyediting: Susana González

Layout & Pre-press: Ignasi Gracia Blanco

Translations: Ana Cristina G. Cañizares (English), Martin Fischer (German) Michel Ficerai / Lingo Sense (French), Grazia Suffritti (Italian)

Produced by Loft Publications
www.loftpublications.com

Published by teNeues Publishing Group

teNeues Publishing Company
16 West 22nd Street, New York, NY 10010, USA
Tel.: 001-212-627-9090, Fax: 001-212-627-9511

teNeues Book Division
Kaistraße 18
40221 Düsseldorf, Germany
Tel.: 0049-(0)211-994597-0, Fax: 0049-(0)211-994597-40

teNeues Publishing UK Ltd.
P.O. Box 402
West Byfleet
KT14 7ZF, Great Britain
Tel.: 0044-1932-403509, Fax: 0044-1932-403514

teNeues France S.A.R.L.
4, rue de Valence
75005 Paris, France
Tel.: 0033-1-55 76 62 05, Fax: 0033-1-55 76 64 19

www.teneues.com

ISBN: 3-8238-4586-1

© 2004 teNeues Verlag GmbH + Co. KG, Kempen

Printed in Germany

Bibliographic information published by
Die Deutsche Bibliothek. Die Deutsche Bibliothek lists
this publication in the Deutsche Nationalbibliografie;
detailed bibliographic data is available in the Internet
at http://dnb.ddb.de.

Contents

Introducción

El entusiasmo de Barcelona por el diseño se hace tangible en casi todos los luga-
res de la ciudad, y especialmente en los restaurantes. Desde los locales de anta-
ño, donde el recuerdo del pasado se materializa en una decoración muy cuidada,
con antigüedades y utensilios de cocina de época, hasta los restaurantes recien-
temente inaugurados, en los que las últimas tendencias en arquitectura e interio-
rismo conforman ambientes exclusivos para degustar los diferentes platos, un festival no sólo para el paladar sino también para los demás sentidos.

La fijación y el esmero en todos los aspectos del diseño han llevado a los restau-
radores a escoger muy cuidadosamente todos los elementos que forman parte
del local, tanto los elementos constructivos y decorativos como las vajillas y cris-
talerías en las que se sirven los productos. Además, el emplatado de la comida
es igual de importante que su exquisitez: la distribución de los alimentos en el
plato, la composición de formas, texturas y tonalidades.

El legado de la tradición culinaria catalana también es uno de los aspectos que la
mayoría de los restaurantes barceloneses miman con orgullo. Ya sea a través de
la reproducción de recetas antiguas, incluso de algunas que datan de la Edad
Media y que han perdurado a través de los siglos, ya sea a partir de la reinterpre-
tación imaginativa de platos típicos como pueden ser la crema catalana, el pan
con tomate o los guisos de aves.

Por otra parte, los restaurantes internacionales han ido estableciéndose en la ciudad, si bien al principio predominaban los restaurantes asiáticos, en la actualidad
ya se puede gozar de excelentes comidas de todo el mundo. Asimismo, la fusión
de estas cocinas también ha dado sugerentes frutos.

Este volumen recoge una cuidada selección de restaurantes que destacan por su
calidad y tradición, como el Botafumeiro y el 7 Portes; por su cocina innovadora y
experimental, como Comerç 24 y El Racó d'en Freixa; por el estilo y el glamour,
como el Noti o el Tatí, o por su especial situación a orillas del Mediterráneo, como el Bestial y el CDLC.

Introduction

Barcelona's enthusiasm for design is palpable in nearly every place in the city, and most particularly in its restaurants. From long-established venues where a reminiscence of the past materializes into a décor comprised of antiques and old cooking utensils, to recently opened restaurants whose cutting edge architecture and design generate exclusive environments that offer a variety of cuisines and a feast for all the senses.

The tenacity and care of the design have prompted the restaurateurs to thoughtfully select the elements that were to form part of the space, from constructive elements to more decorative ones, such as the dishware and glassware used to serve the products. In addition, the presentation of each dish is just as important as its exquisiteness: the distribution of food on the plate, along with the composition of forms, textures and colors.

The legacy of traditional Catalán cuisine is another aspect that most Barcelonian restaurants embrace with pride. This may include the recreation of old recipes dating as far back as the Middle Ages that have endured through the centuries, or the imaginative reinterpretacion of typical dishes like the "crema catalana", "pan con tomate", or poultry stews.

The international restaurants that have gradually established themselves in the city have grown from being predominantly Asian-influenced to providing a wide range of excellent cuisines from around the world. Consequently, fusion cuisine has become a popular culinary offer.

This volume gathers a careful selection of restaurants that stand out for their quality and tradition, such as the Botafumeiro and the 7 Portes; for their innovative and experimental cuisine, like the Comerç 24 and the Racó d'en Freixa; for their style and glamour, like the Noti or the Tatí, or for their priveleged location on the shores of the Mediterranean, like the Bestial or the CDLC.

Einleitung

Überall in Barcelona zeigt sich die Vorliebe für ausgefallenes Design, doch ganz besonders gilt dies in den Restaurants. Der Bogen reicht von den traditionsreichen Etablissements, in denen sich die Erinnerung an vergangene Zeiten in der liebevoll gepflegten Einrichtung mit ihren Antiquitäten und ihrem alten Küchengerät ausdrückt, bis hin zu den erst kürzlich eröffneten Häusern, deren exklusives Ambiente von den neuesten Tendenzen der Innenarchitektur bestimmt wird. So verwandelt sich die Gaumenfreude beim Genuss der angebotenen Gerichte in ein wahres Fest der Sinne.

Die Inhaber der Restaurants haben besondere Sorgfalt darauf verwandt, alle Elemente der Ausstattung ihrer Häuser aufeinander abzustimmen, die bauliche Gestaltung und die Dekoration ebenso wie das Geschirr und die Gläser. Und natürlich ist die Präsentation der Gerichte genauso wichtig wie ihre ausgezeichnete Qualität: Beim Servieren wird auf die Anordnung der Zutaten auf dem Teller, auf die Kombination von Formen, Farben und Texturen geachtet.

Ein weiterer Aspekt, auf den die Restaurants in Barcelona stolz sind, ist die kulinarische Tradition Kataloniens. So werden noch heute Gerichte zubereitet, die zum Teil schon seit dem Mittelalter überliefert sind und die Zeitläufte überdauert haben. Doch auf der anderen Seite werden typische katalanische Rezepte auf fantasievolle Weise neu interpretiert, wie z. B. die gebrannte Karamelcreme, das Tomatenbrot oder viele Geflügelgerichte.

Mittlerweile haben sich auch Spezialitätenrestaurants anderer Nationalitäten in der Stadt niedergelassen. Zunächst war vor allem die fernöstliche Küche vertreten, doch heute werden hervorragende Mahlzeiten der verschiedensten Küchentraditionen aus der ganzen Welt angeboten. Und natürlich bringt die gegenseitige Durchdringung dieser unterschiedlichen Traditionen vielversprechende Früchte hervor.

In dem vorliegenden Band findet sich eine Auswahl von Restaurants, die sich einmal durch ihre Qualität und Tradition auszeichnen, wie Botafumeiro oder 7 Portes, oder solche, die durch ihre ausgefallene experimentelle Küche auf sich aufmerksam machen, wie Comerç 24 oder Racó d'en Freixa, dann andere, die durch Stil und Glamour glänzen, wie Noti oder Tatí, und schließlich Häuser, die durch ihre aufsehenerregende Lage am Mittelmeer von sich reden machen, wie Bestial oder CDLC.

Introduction

L'enthousiasme de Barcelone envers le design est tangible dans pratiquement chaque recoin de la cité et particulièrement dans ses restaurants. Des restaurants à l'ancienne où le souvenir du passé se matérialise par le biais d'une décoration soignée – antiquités et ustensiles de cuisine d'époque – jusqu'aux sites les plus contemporains voyant les dernières tendances architecturales et d'intérieur former des atmosphères exclusives pour déguster les différents plats, c'est un festival non seulement du goût mais interpellant également les autres sens.

L'obsession du design et l'attention portée à chacun de ses aspects ont conduit les restaurateurs à choisir avec un soin extrême les éléments formant le lieu, tant les composants relatifs à la décoration et à la décoration que la vaisselle et la verrerie dans lesquels les mets sont servis. Par surcroît, la présentation de plats remplit un rôle aussi important que leur raffinement : la distribution des aliments dans le plat, la composition des formes, textures et tonalités.

L'héritage de la tradition culinaire catalane constitue également un des aspects que la plupart des restaurants barcelonais cultivent avec fierté. Que ce soit en reproduisant des recettes du temps jadis, notamment certaines du Moyen âge ayant perduré au fil des siècles, ou en choisissant de revisiter avec imagination des plats typiques comme peuvent l'être la crème catalane, le pain à la tomate ou les plats de volaille.

Par ailleurs, les restaurants internationaux ont commencé à prendre pied dans la cité. Bien que les restaurants asiatiques aient pu dominer au départ, il est aujourd'hui possible de se délecter d'excellentes cuisines du monde entier. De même, la fusion de ces cuisines a porté des fruits délicieux.

Cet ouvrage recueille une sélection de restaurants choisis avec soin, remarquables par leur qualité et leurs traditions – ainsi le Botafumeiro et le 7 Portes – leur cuisine novatrice et expérimentale – ainsi le Comerç 24 et le Racó d'en Freixa – leur style et leur glamour – ainsi le Noti ou le Tatí – ou enfin leur situation sur les rives de la Méditerranée – ainsi le Bestial et le CDLC.

Introduzione

L'entusiasmo di Barcellona per il design é tangibile in quasi tutti i luoghi della cittá, e specialmente nei ristoranti. Partendo dai locali di sempre, dove il ricordo del passato si materializza in un arredamento molto attento, con oggetti antichi e vecchi utensili da cucina, fino ai ristoranti inaugurati di recente, nei quali le ultime tendenze in architettura e design hanno dato forma ad ambienti esclusivi per la degustazione dei diversi piatti, un festival non solo per il palato ma anche per tutti gli altri sensi.

L'ossessione e lo sforzo in tutti gli aspetti della progettazione hanno portato i ristoranti a scegliere con molta attenzione tutti gli elementi che fanno parte del locale, sia gli elementi costruttivi e decorativi, che i servizi di piatti e bicchieri nei quali servono i prodotti. La presentazione del cibo é diventata inoltre tanto importante come la sua squisitezza: la distribuzione degli alimenti nel piatto e la composizione di forme, superfici e tonalitá sono elementi fondamentali.

Uno degli aspetti che la maggior parte dei ristoranti di Barcellona rispettano con orgoglio é la tradizione culinaria catalana. Sia attraverso la proposta di ricette antiche, incluso alcune medievali che si sono mantenute attraverso i secoli, sia partendo dalla reinterpretazione fantasiosa di piatti tipici, come la crema catalana, il pane e pomodoro o gli stufati di pollame.

D'altra parte, anche i ristoranti internazionali si sono stabiliti poco a poco in cittá, e se all'inizio erano predominanti i ristoranti asiatici, attualmente si possono gustare eccellenti piatti provenienti da tutto il mondo. Allo stesso modo, la fusione di queste cucine ha dato frutti suggestivi.

Questo volume raccoglie un'attenta selezione dei ristoranti che emergono per la loro qualitá e tradizione, come il Botafumeiro e il 7 Portes; per la loro cucina innovativa e sperimentale, come il Comerç 24 e il Racó d'en Freixa; per lo stile e il glamour, come il Noti o il Tatí, o per la loro speciale situazione geografica sulle rive del Mediterraneo come il Bestial e il CDLC.

9

Passeig Isabel II 14 | 08003 Barcelona
Phone: +34 933 193 033
www.7portes.com
Subway: Barceloneta
Opening hours: Everyday 1 pm to 1 am
Average price: € 30
Cuisine: Catalan
Special features: Housed in a building that is national monument, well-stocked cellar

Buñuelos

de bacalao

Codfish Fritters

Stockfischbällchen

Beignets de morue

Frittelle di baccalà

200 g de morro de bacalao en remojo
1 patata
200 ml de agua de la cocción del bacalao
200 g de harina
75 g de manteca de cerdo
2–3 huevos
3 dientes de ajo
Perejil
Aceite
Sal y pimienta

Poner el bacalao en un recipiente cubierto de agua para que se caliente (sin hervir). Una vez cocido, apartar el agua. Limpiar de espinas y piel y picar en el mortero.

Poner al fuego el agua de la cocción junto con la manteca. Una vez haya arrancado a hervir, añadir la harina y remover continuadamente con una varilla.
Cuando se ha obtenido una mezcla compacta, apartar del fuego, añadir los huevos y mezclar bien. Agregar a la masa el bacalao, los ajos y el perejil, éstos últimos picados también en el mortero. Mezclar de nuevo y sazonar con sal y pimienta.
Freír en abundante aceite con ayuda de una cuchara de postre.

7 oz of soaked codfish snout
1 potato
200 ml of water used to cook codfish
7 oz flour
2 1/2 oz lard
2–3 eggs
3 cloves of garlic
Parsley
Olive oil
Salt, pepper

Place codfish in a pot and cover with water until hot (without boiling). Once cooked, remove water and set aside. Remove skin and bones and mince with a mortar.
Mix water and lard and bring to a boil, add flour and stir continuously with wooden spoon.
Once the mix has thickened, remove from the fire, add eggs and mix well. Add codfish and ground garlic and parsley to the dough, mix and season with salt and pepper. Fry in abundant oil with the help of a dessert spoon.

200 g eingeweichter Stockfisch
1 Kartoffel
200 ml Wasser (Stockfischsud)
200 g Mehl
75 g Schweineschmalz
2–3 Eier
3 Knoblauchzehen
Petersilie
Öl
Salz, Pfeffer

Den Stockfisch in einem mit Wasser gefüllten Deckeltopf erhitzen (nicht kochen). Das Wasser abgießen und beiseite stellen. Den Fisch entgräten und im Mörser zerstampfen.

Den Stockfischsud mit dem Schmalz erhitzen. Sobald das Wasser kocht, unter ständigem Rühren mit einem Holzlöffel das Mehl hinzugeben. Wenn eine feste Masse entstanden ist, von der Kochstelle nehmen, die Eier dazugeben und gut verrühren. Dann den Stockfisch und den Knoblauch und die Petersilie hinzufügen, die zuvor ebenfalls im Mörser zerstoßen worden sind. Noch einmal umrühren und mit Salz und Pfeffer abschmecken.
Mit Hilfe eines Teelöffels kleine Bällchen formen und in reichlich Öl braten.

200 g de museau de morue mariné
1 pomme de terre
200 ml d'eau de cuisson de la morue
200 g de farine
75 g de lard
2–3 œufs
3 pointes d'ail
Persil
Huile
Sel, poivre

Placez la morue couverte d'eau dans un récipient pour la chauffer (sans ébullition). Une fois cuite, réserver l'eau. Retirer peau et arêtes et hacher dans un mortier.

Placer sur le feu l'eau de cuisson avec le lard. Dès l'ébullition, ajouter la farine et remuer sans arrêt avec un bâtonnet.
À obtention d'une masse compacte, retirer du feu, ajouter les œufs et bien incorporer. Ajouter la morue à la masse avec l'ail et le persil, ces derniers également hachés au mortier. Mélanger de nouveau et assaisonner avec du sel et du poivre.
Frire dans l'huile abondante à l'aide d'une cuillère à dessert.

200 g di baccalà dissalato e ammorbidito
1 patata
200 ml di acqua di cottura del baccalà
200 g di farina
75 g di strutto
2–3 uova
3 denti di aglio
Prezzemolo
Olio
Sale, pepe

Mettere il baccalà in una pentola con acqua sufficiente a coprirlo per riscaldarlo (senza arrivare al bollore). Quando è cotto scolarlo, diliscarlo, togliere la pelle e sminuzzarlo in un mortaio.
Scaldare l'acqua di cottura con lo strutto. Quando comincia a bollire aggiungere la farina e muovere senza interruzione con un cucchiaio di legno. Quando il composto è compatto, toglierlo dal fuoco, aggiungere le uova e mescolare bene. Aggiungere al miscuglio il baccalà e l'aglio e il prezzemolo tritati nel mortaio. Mescolare di nuovo e aggiungere sale e pepe.
Friggere in abbondante olio con l'aiuto di un cucchiaio da dolci.

Phone: +34 933 196 600
www.restaurantabac.biz
Subway: Barceloneta
Opening hours: Everyday 1:30 pm to 4 pm, and 8:30 pm to 11 pm
Average price: € 95
Cuisine: Creative
Special features: Honoured with a Michelin star

Tartar de buey
de mar con aguacate

Crab Tartar with Avocado

Tartar von Taschenkrebsen mit Avocado

Tartare de tourteau à l'avocat

Tartara di granciporro con avocado

---

2 bueyes de mar de 600 g
1 aguacate
6 champiñones de París
1 escalonia
4 cucharaditas de caviar
Hierbas picadas: ajipuerro, perejil
Pimienta, polvo de pimiento del piquillo
Aceite de hierbas, zumo de limón
Aceite, vinagre, mostaza y sal de Guérande

Hervir los bueyes de mar (calcular 14 minutos
de cocción por cada 800 g de peso del animal).
Refrescar con agua y hielo, y extraer la carne.

Vinagreta: Mezclar mostaza, sal, pimienta y
vinagre en un bol y añadir aceite.
Guarnición: Picar los champiñones y medio
aguacate, disponerlos en un bol y añadir parte
de la vinagreta y unas gotas de zumo de limón.
Seguidamente, incorporar algo de las hierbas, el
polvo de pimiento y la escalonia picada.
Por otro lado, poner la carne del marisco y el
resto de la vinagreta en otro bol. Mezclar y añadir el resto de las hierbas. Finalmente disponer
en un molde redondo una capa de guarnición y
otra de carne de buey. Desmoldar y decorar con
medio aguacate y caviar.

---

2 crabs (21 oz each)
1 avocado
6 Parisian mushrooms
1 scallion
4 tsp of caviar
Chopped herbs: leek, parsley
Pepper, red pepper powder
Herb-marinated oil, lemon juice
Oil, vinegar, mustard and Guérande salt

Boil crabs (calculate 14 minutes cooking time
per 28 oz of weight). Cool down with water and
ice, and extract the meat.

Vinaigrette: Mix mustard, sal, pepper and vinegar in a bowl and add oil.
Garnish: Chop mushrooms and half an avocado,
place in a bowl and add part of the vinaigrette
and several drops of lemon juice. Next, add
some of the herbs, red pepper powder and
chopped scallion.
Separately, place the crabmeat and rest of the
vinaigrette in another bowl. Mix and add the remaining herbs. Finally, place a layer of garnish
and the crabmeat in a round mold. Turn over to
remove from mold and decorate with half an avocado and caviar.

2 Taschenkrebse zu je 600 g
1 Avocado
6 Pariser Champignons
1 Schalotte
4 TL Kaviar
Gehackte Kräuter: Wilder Lauch, Petersilie
Pfeffer, Paprikapulver, Zitronensaft, Kräuteröl
Öl, Essig, Senf und Meersalz aus Guérande

Die Taschenkrebse kochen (man rechnet 14
Minuten je 800 g Gewicht). Mit Wasser und Eis
abkühlen und das Fleisch herauslösen.
Vinaigrette: Senf, Salz, Pfeffer und Essig vermischen und Öl dazugeben.

Garnierung: Champignons und eine halbe Avocado zerkleinern, in eine Schüssel geben, einen
Teil der Vinaigrette und ein paar Tropfen
Zitronensaft beifügen. Anschließend etwas von
den Kräutern, das Paprikapulver und die
gehackte Schalotte dazugeben.
Das Krebsfleisch und den Rest der Vinaigrette in
eine andere Schüssel geben, vermischen und
die restlichen Kräuter dazugeben. Schließlich
eine runde Form mit einer Schicht der Garnierung auslegen, dann das Krebsfleisch darüber verteilen. Stürzen und mit der halben
Avocado und Kaviar garnieren.

2 tourteaux de 600 g
1 avocat
6 champignons de Paris
1 échalote
4 c. à café de caviar
Herbes hachées : poireau d'été, persil
Poivre, poivrons « del piquillo » en poudre
Huile d'herbes, jus de citron
Huile, vinaigre, moutarde et sel de Guérande

Faire bouillir les tourteaux (calculer 14 minutes
de cuisson pour chaque 800 g de crustacé). Ra-
fraîchir avec de l'eau et de la glace et extraire la
chair.

Vinaigrette : Mélanger moutarde, sel, poivre et
vinaigre dans un bol et ajouter l'huile.
Garniture : Hacher les champignons et la moitié
de l'avocat, les disposer dans un bol et ajouter
une partie de la vinaigrette plus quelques gouttes de citron. Ensuite, incorporer un peu des
herbes, le poivron moulu et l'échalote hachée.
Par ailleurs, disposer la chair des tourteaux et
le reste de la vinaigrette dans un bol. Mélanger
et ajouter le reste des herbes. Disposer finalement dans un moule rond une couche de garniture avec la chair des tourteaux. Démouler et
décorer avec le demi avocat et le caviar.

2 granciporo da 600 g
1 avocado
6 champignon di Parigi
1 scalogno
4 cucchicini di caviale
Erbe aromatiche tritate: porro selvatico, prezzemolo
Pepe, paprica, olio d'erbe, succo di limone
Olio, aceto, senape e sale di Guérande

Lessare i granciporo (calcolare 14 minuti di cottura ogni 800 g di peso). Raffreddarli in acqua e
ghiaccio ed estrarre la polpa.

Vinagrette: Mescolare senape, sale, pepe e aceto in una tazza ed aggiungere l'olio.
Guarnizione: Tritare gli champignon e mezzo avocado, metterli in una ciotola ed aggiungere parte della vinagrette e qualche goccia di limone.
Quindi spolverarli con un poco di erbe aromatiche, la paprica e lo scalogno tritato.
Mettere la polpa del crostaceo ed il resto della
vinagrette in un'altra ciotola. Mescolare ed aggiungere il resto delle erbe. Alla fine sistemare
in uno stampo rotondo uno strato di guarnizione
e la polpa di granciporro. Togliere dallo stampo
e decorare con l'avocado rimasto e il caviale.

Aqua

Design: Sandra Tarruella, Isabel López |
Chef: Evaristo Triano

Passeig Marítim 30 | 08003 Barcelona
Phone: +34 932 251 272
www.aguadeltragaluz.com
Subway: Barceloneta
Opening hours: Everyday 1:30 pm to 4 pm (Sat and Sun to 5 pm), and 8:30 pm to
midnight (Fri and Sat to 1 am)
Average price: € 25
Cuisine: Marine
Special features: Terrace on the beach, spectacular views of the sea

Arroz
con alcachofas y sepia

Rice with Artichokes and Cuttlefish

Reis mit Artischocken und Tintenfisch

Riz aux artichauts et à la seiche

Riso con carciofi e seppia

1/2 kg de arroz
1 kg de sepia fresca
1/2 kg de colas de gamba
1 kg de alcachofas
1/2 kg de cebollas
1/2 kg de pimiento rojo
1/2 kg de tomate natural
250 ml de aceite de oliva
Caldo de pescado

Poner el aceite de oliva en una sartén, añadir las cebollas troceadas y el pimiento y rehogar.

Seguidamente agregar la sepia cortada en trozos de tamaño mediano y medio vaso de agua y cocer unas dos horas aproximadamente. Si es necesario, puede echarse algo más de agua para que no se pegue. Pasado este tiempo, añadir el tomate y dejar media hora más.
En otra sartén saltear las colas de gamba con un poco de aceite; después echar el arroz, la sepia y las alcachofas troceadas y añadir el caldo de pescado.
Trasladar todo a una cazuela de barro para terminar la cocción en el horno de carbón.

1 lb rice
2 lb fresh cuttlefish
1 lb shrimp tails
2 lb artichokes
1 lb onions
1 lb red pepper
1 lb natural tomato
250 ml of olive oil
Fish stock

Place olive oil in a pan, and sauté chopped onions and peppers. Next, add medium-sized

pieces of cuttlefish and half a glass of water and leave to cook for approximately two hours. If necessary, add more water to avoid sticking. Afterward, add tomato and leave another half hour to cook.
In another pan, fry the shrimp tails with a bit of oil, then throw in the rice, cuttlefish, chopped artichokes and fish stock.
Transfer the contents into a ceramic pot to finish the cooking inside a charcoal oven.

1/2 kg Reis
1 kg frischer Tintenfisch (Sepia)
1/2 kg Garnelenschwänze
1 kg Artischocken
1/2 kg Zwiebeln
1/2 kg rote Paprikaschoten
1/2 kg geschälte Tomaten
250 ml Olivenöl
Fischbrühe

Das Olivenöl in eine Pfanne gießen und die kleingeschnittenen Zwiebeln und Paprikaschoten darin braten. Den in mittelgroße Stücke geschnittenen Tintenfisch und ein halbes Glas Wasser dazugeben und etwa zwei Stunden lang schmoren. Falls erforderlich, noch etwas Wasser nachgießen, damit es nicht anbrennt. Dann die Tomaten beigeben und noch eine halbe Stunde schmoren lassen.
In einer anderen Pfanne die Garnelenschwänze in ein wenig Öl anbraten, den Reis, den Tintenfisch und die zerkleinerten Artischocken und die Fischbrühe dazugeben.
Alles in eine irdene Schüssel geben und im Backofen fertig garen lassen.

1/2 kg de riz
1 kg de seiche fraîche
1/2 kg de queues de crevettes
1 kg d'artichauts
1/2 kg d'oignons
1/2 kg de poivrons rouges
1/2 kg de jus de tomate naturel
250 ml d'huile d'olive
Bouillon de poisson

Verser l'huile dans une poêle, ajouter les oignons en lamelles et les poivrons puis faire sauter. Ajouter ensuite la seiche en morceaux de taille moyenne et un demi verre d'eau puis laisser cuire environ deux heures. Si nécessaire, il est possible d'ajouter un peu d'eau en cours de cuisson pour éviter d'attacher. À la fin de la cuisson, ajouter le jus de tomate et poursuivre la cuisson d'une demie heure.
Dans une autre poêle, faire sauter les queues de crevettes dans un peu d'huile. Ajouter ensuite le riz, la seiche et les artichauts en morceaux puis le bouillon de poisson.
Transférer le tout dans une terrine en terre cuite pour terminer la cuisson dans un fournil.

1/2 kg di riso
1 kg di seppia fresca
1/2 kg di code di gambero
1 kg di carciofi
1/2 kg di cipolle
1/2 kg di peperoni rossi
1/2 kg di pomodori
250 ml di olio d'oliva
Brodo di pesce

Rosolare in una padella le cipolle tritate e i peperoni con un po' d'olio. Quindi aggiungere la seppia tagliata a pezzi non troppo piccoli con mezzo bicchiere d'acqua e lasciar cuocere due ore circa. Se necessario, aggiungere un po' d'acqua per evitare che si attacchi. Passato il tempo indicato aggiungere i pomodori e lasciar cuocere un'altra mezz'ora.
In un'altra padella rosolare le code di gambero in un po' d'olio, quindi aggiungere il riso, la seppia e i carciofi tagliati a pezzi aggiungendo il brodo di pesce.
Passare il tutto in una pentola di coccio per terminare la cottura nel forno a legna.

Bestial

Design: Sandra Tarruella, Isabel López |
Chef: Samuel G. Galdón

Carrer de Ramon Trias Fargas 2-4 | 08005 Barcelona
Phone: +34 932 240 407
www.bestialdeltragaluz.com
Subway: Bogatell
Opening hours: Everyday 1:30 pm to 4 pm (Fri–Sun to 5 pm), and 8:30 pm to 1 am
Average price: € 30
Cuisine: Italian
Special features: Live music, video-jockeys, disc jockeys, in front of the sea

Arroz de codorniz
y gamba de Palamós

Quail and Palamós Shrimp Rice

Wachtelreis mit Garnelen aus Palamós

Riz de cailles et crevette de palamós

Riso di quaglia e gambero di Palamós

1 codorniz de tiro
60 g de cebolla
100 g de arroz bomba
60 g de caldo oscuro de codorniz
20 g de mantequilla
20 g de queso parmesano
1 gamba de Palamós de 200 g
50 ml de caldo de crustáceos reducido
Sal y pimienta recién molida

Sofreír la cebolla previamente troceada hasta que quede completamente transparente; añadir el arroz y remover a la vez que se añade el caldo de codorniz de manera que quede un acabado de risotto. Una vez se haya evaporado el caldo, montar con mantequilla y parmesano.
Saltear la gamba hasta obtener un tono rosado junto con la codorniz, todo en la misma sartén para que los jugos se mezclen. Reservar.
Disponer en un plato el arroz, la gamba y la codorniz deshuesada. Presentar el caldo de crustáceos en una jarrita aparte para que el comensal se sirva a su gusto.

1 quail
2 oz onions
3 1/2 oz of medium-grained rice
2 oz of dark quail broth
1/2 oz of butter
1/2 oz of Parmesan cheese
1 Palamós shrimp (7 oz)
50 ml of reduced shellfish stock
Salt, freshly ground pepper

Lightly fry the previously chopped onion until transparent. Add rice and stir while gradually introducing the quail broth to obtain a risotto finish. When the broth has been absorbed, mix in butter and Parmesan cheese.
Sauté the shrimp until rosy along with the quail in the same pan so that the juices mix. Set aside.
Place the rice, shrimp and boned quail on a plate. Place shellfish stock in a separate jug and serve to taste.

1 Wachtel
60 g Zwiebeln
100 g rundkörniger Reis
60 g dunkle Wachtelbrühe
20 g Butter
20 g Parmesan
1 Garnele aus Palamós (200 g)
50 ml konzentrierte Krustentierbrühe
Salz und frisch gemahlener Pfeffer

Zwiebel hacken und glasig braten, den Reis und unter ständigem Rühren die Wachtelbrühe hinzu-

geben, bis ein Risotto entsteht. Sobald die Flüssigkeit aufgebraucht ist, mit Butter und Käse bekrönen.
Die Garnele und die Wachtel in einer Pfanne golden anbraten, sodass sich der Sud vermischt. Beiseite stellen.
Auf einem Teller den Reis, die Garnele und das von den Knochen gelöste Wachtelfleisch arrangieren. Die Krustentierbrühe in einer Sauciere bereit stellen, damit sich jeder nach Geschmack davon nehmen kann.

1 caille sylvestre
60 g d'oignon
100 g de riz rond
60 g de bouillon de caille
20 g de beurre
20 g de parmesan
1 crevette de Palamós de 200 g
50 ml de bouillon de crustacés réduit
Sel et poivre fraîchement moulu

Faire sauter l'oignon préalablement coupée pour le rendre translucide complètement ; ajouter le

riz et remuer tout en ajoutant le bouillon de caille pour finir un peu en risotto. Lors que le bouillon soi arrivé a la temperture de évaporation du bouillon, monter avec le beurre et le parmesan.
Faire sauter la crevette pour la faire rosir avec la caille, dans la même poêle afin que les jus se mêlent. Réserver.
Disposer dans un plat le riz, la crevette et la caille désossée. Servir le bouillon de crustacés dans une saucière à part afin de se servir à son goût.

1 quaglia di cacciaggione
60 g de cipolla
100 g de riso
60 g di brodo denso di quaglia
20 g de burro
20 g di parmigiano
1 gambero di Palamós da 200 g
50 ml di brodo di crostacei ridotto
Sale e pepe appena macinato

Soffriggere la cipolla anzitutto tagliata finchè diventano trasparenti; aggiungere il riso e mescolare mentre si aggiunge il brodo di quaglia come per fare un risotto. A fine cottura mantecare con burro e parmigiano.
Rosolare il gambero finchè non prende un tono rosato, nella stessa padella con la quaglia perchè si mescolino i sughi. Mettere da parte.
Disporre in un piatto il riso, il gambero e la quaglia disossata. Servire il brodo di crostacei in una piccola brocca a parte perché il commensale si serva direttamente.

Carrer Gran de Gràcia 81 | 08012 Barcelona
Phone: +34 932 184 230
www.botafumeiro.es
Subway: Fontana
Opening hours: Everyday 1 pm to 1 am
Average price: € 30 – € 60
Cuisine: Marine
Special features: Probably the best Galician restaurant of the world

Botafumeiro | **31**

Surtido

de mariscos

Seafood Platter

Verschiedene Meeresfrüchte

Plateau de fruits de mer

Assortimento di frutti di mare

5 ostras
1/2 kg de almejas
1/2 kg percebes
2 centollos de 400 g
1/2 kg de langostinos
1/2 kg de gambas
Cebolla y laurel
Limón y perejil

Hervir en abundante agua de mar y por separado los percebes, los centollos, las gambas y los langostinos. Para potenciar su sabor, añadir al agua cebolla y un hoja de laurel.

Una vez fríos, descarnar los centollos, a excepción de las patas, y picar la carne junto con las entrañas. Aliñar al gusto. Presentar la mezcla en la propia cáscara del centollo junto a las patas enteras.
Emplatado: Disponer en una fuente grande los centollos, y las gambas y los langostinos pelados sin haber separado el cuerpo de la cabeza. Los percebes se sirven enteros. Las ostras y las almejas se presentan vivas y abiertas listas para aliñar con limón.

5 oysters
1 lb clams
1 lb barnacles
2 spider crabs (14 oz each)
1 lb king prawns
1 lb shrimp
Onion and bay leaves
Lemon and parsley

Boil separately the barnacles, spider crabs, shrimp and prawns in abundant sea water. To enhance their flavor, add onion and one bay leaf to the water.

Once cold, extract the meat from the spider crabs, except for the legs, and mince the meat together with the entrails. Season to taste. Present the mix inside the crab shells with the legs. To serve: Place the spider crabs in a large platter, along with the peeled shrimp and prawns without removing the heads. The barnacles are served whole. The oysters and clams are served alive and open, ready to season with lemon.

5 Austern
1/2 kg Venusmuscheln
1/2 kg Entenmuscheln
2 Seespinnen zu je 400 g
1/2 kg Langostinos
1/2 kg Garnelen
Zwiebel und Lorbeer
Zitrone und Petersilie

Die Entenmuscheln, Seespinnen, Langostinos und Garnelen getrennt voneinander in reichlich Meerwasser kochen. Zur Verstärkung des Eigengeschmacks Zwiebel und Lorbeerblätter ins Wasser tun.

Nach dem Abkühlen das Fleisch der Seespinnen herauslösen, aber die Beine ganz lassen. Das Fleisch zusammen mit den Innereien zerkleinern. Nach Geschmack würzen. In der Seespinnenschale servieren und die Beine dazulegen.
Serviervorschlag: Seespinnen, Garnelen und Langostinos (ohne den Kopf abzutrennen) auf einen Servierteller legen. Die Entenmuscheln werden ganz serviert. Die lebenden Austern und Venusmuscheln geöffnet servieren, so dass man sie mit Zitrone beträufeln kann.

5 huîtres
1/2 kg de palourdes
1/2 kg de pouces-pieds
2 crabes de 400 g
1/2 kg de langoustines
1/2 kg de crevettes
Oignon et laurier
Citron et persil

Faire bouillir dans de l'eau de mer en abondance et séparément les pouces-pieds, les crabes, les crevettes et les langoustines. Pour renforcer la saveur, ajouter l'oignon et une feuille de laurier dans l'eau.

Une fois refroidis, extraire la chair des crabes, sauf les pattes, et la hacher avec les entrailles. Assaisonner selon les goûts. Présenter le mélange dans la carapace même du crabe, avec les pattes entières.
Présentation : Disposer dans un grand plat creux les crabes accompagnés des crevettes et des langoustines décortiquées sans séparer le corps de la tête. Les pouces-pieds sont servis entiers. Les huîtres et les palourdes se présentent vivent et ouvertes, prêtes à être assaisonnées de citron.

5 ostriche
1/2 kg di vongole
1/2 kg lepadi
2 granseole da 400 g
1/2 kg di gamberoni
1/2 kg di gamberi
Cipolla e alloro
Limone e prezzemolo

Bollire in abbondante acqua di mare e separatamente i lepadi, le granseole, i gamberi e i gamberoni. Per potenziare il sapore, aggiungere all'acqua la cipolla e una foglia d'alloro.

Quando si sono raffreddati, togliere la polpa alle granseole, eccetto le zampe, e tritare la carne insieme a l'interiora. Condire a piacere. Mettere la polpa nello stesso guscio della granseola insieme alle zampe intere.
Presentazione: Disporre in un piatto da portata grande le granseole, i gamberi e i gamberoni pelati senza separare il corpo dalle teste. I lepadi vanno serviti interi. Le ostriche e le vongole si presentano vive e aperte per essere condite con limone.

Cacao Sampaka

Design: Antoni Arola I Chefs: Quim Capdevila, Ramón Morató, Albert Adrià

Carrer Consell de Cent 292 I 08007 Barcelona
Phone: +34 932 720 833
www.cacaosampaka.com
Subway: Passeig de Gràcia
Opening hours: Everyday 9 am to 8:30 pm, Sun 5 pm to 8:30 pm
Cuisine: Chocolate Shop
Special features: Great and imaginative selection of chocolates

CDLC Barcelona

Design: Jaime Romano | Chef: Raúl Querol

Passeig Marítim 32 | 08005 Barcelona
Phone: +34 932 240 470
www.cdlcbarcelona.com
info@cdlcbarcelona.com
Subway: Ciutadella
Opening hours: Everyday midday to 3 am
Average price: € 20 – € 30
Cuisine: International
Special features: Terrace on the beach, club and lounge with views of the sea

Bogavante
mediterráneo

Mediterranean Lobster

Hummer auf mediterrane Art

Homard à la méditerranéenne

Astice mediterraneo

10 mejillones
5 almejas grandes
10 percebes
1/2 bogavante
3 ajos tiernos
Aceite de oliva
Aceite de girasol
Sal y pimienta en grano
Laurel
Vinagre de Jerez

Limpiar los mejillones y los percebes y cocer por separado. Cocer también las almejas al vapor.

Una vez fríos se separan de la concha, a excepción de los percebes, que se reservan enteros. En una cazuela poner la carne de los mejillones, percebes y almejas y cubrir con aceite de oliva y aceite de girasol en proporciones idénticas. Laminar los ajos tiernos y añadirlos a la cazuela junto con el laurel, y sal y pimienta al gusto. Dejar a fuego lento sin que el aceite llegue a ebullición durante 10 minutos. Añadir un chorro de vinagre de Jerez y dejar reposar.
Marcar a la plancha el bogavante. Disponerlo en un plato y esparcir sobre él la mezcla de crustáceos previamente escurrida. Decorar con los percebes.

10 mussels
5 large clams
10 barnacles
1/2 a lobster
3 young garlic
Olive oil
Sunflower oil
Salt and peppercorns
Bay leaves
Sherry vinegar

Wash the mussels and the barnacles and boil separately. Steam the clams.

Once cool, separate from the shell, except for the barnacles. In one pot, cover the mussels, barnacles and clams in olive oil and sunflower oil in identical proportions.
Slice the garlic and add to the pot, along with the bay leaves, salt and pepper.
Leave on low heat without bringing the oil to a boil for 10 minutes. Drizzle with Sherry vinegar and allow to settle.
Sear the lobster on the grill. Place on a plate and spread the previously strained shellfish mixture over it, adorning with barnacles.

10 Miesmuscheln
5 große Venusmuscheln
10 Entenmuscheln
1/2 Hummer
3 frische Knoblauchzehen
Olivenöl
Sonnenblumenöl
Salz und Pfefferkörner
Lorbeer
Sherryessig

Miesmuscheln und Entenmuscheln säubern und separat kochen. Die Venusmuscheln dünsten. Die Muscheln nach dem Abkühlen aus den Schalen nehmen, die Entenmuscheln jedoch ganz lassen. Das Fleisch der Mies- und Venusmuscheln und die Entenmuscheln in einen Topf geben und mit Oliven- und Sonnenblumenöl zu gleichen Teilen auffüllen.
Den Knoblauch pressen und mit Lorbeer, Salz und Pfeffer nach Geschmack in den Topf geben Zehn Minuten lang erhitzen, aber nicht kochen. Einen Schuss Sherryessig hinzugeben und ziehen lassen.
Den Hummer auf der heißen Metallplatte anbraten. Auf einen Teller legen und die abgetropfte Muschelmischung darüber verteilen. Mit den Entenmuscheln garnieren.

10 moules
5 grandes palourdes
10 pouces-pieds
1/2 homard
3 pointes d'ail tendre
Huile d'olive
Huile de tournesol
Sel et poivre en grain
Laurier
Vinaigre de Xérès

Laver les moules et les pouces-pieds et les cuire séparément. Cuire également les palourdes à la vapeur.
Une fois refroidis, les séparer de la coquille, sauf pour les pouces-pieds, réservés entiers.
Dans une casserole, placer la chair des moules, des pouces-pieds et des palourdes et couvrir d'huile d'olive et d'huile de tournesol en proportions égales.
Émincer les pointes d'ail tendre et les ajouter dans la casserole avec le laurier, le sel et le poivre, selon les goûts.
Laisser cuire à feu doux, sans que l'huile atteigne l'ébullition, durant 10 minutes. Ajouter une trait de vinaigre de Xérès et laisser reposer.
Marquer le homard au grill. Disposer dans un plat et parsemer de l'assortiment de crustacés, égouttés au préalable. Décorer avec les pouces-pieds.

10 cozze
5 vongole grandi
10 lepadi
1/2 astice
3 germogli d'aglio giovane
Olio d'oliva
Olio di girasole
Sale e pepe in grani
Alloro
Aceto di Jerez

Pulire le cozze e i lepadi e cuocerli separatamente. Cuocere anche le vongole al vapore.
Quando si sono raffreddati si separano dalla conchiglia, esclusi i lepadi che si mettono da parte interi. In una casseruola mettere la polpa delle cozze, i lepadi e le vongole con olio d'oliva e di girasole in proporzioni identiche.
Tagliare a fettine i germogli d'aglio e aggiungerli nella casseruola insieme all'alloro, sale e pepe. Lasciar cuocere a fuoco lento senza che l'olio arrivi a bollire per 10 minuti. Aggiungere una spruzzata di aceto di Jerez e lasciar riposare.
Passare l'astice sulla piastra. Metterlo in un piatto e cospargerlo con la miscela di crostacei previamente scolata. Decorare con i lepadi.

Comerç 24

Design: Alfons Tost | Chef: Carles Abellán

Carrer Comerç 24 | 08003 Barcelona
Phone: +34 933 192 102
www.comerc24.com
Subway: Arc de Triomf, Barceloneta
Opening hours: Everyday 1:30 pm to 3:30 pm, and 8 pm to midnight
Average price: € 42
Cuisine: Creative
Special features: Sumptuous interiors, reinterpretation of traditional cuisine

Salmón & Salmón

Salmon & Salmon

Lachs & Lachs

Saumon & Saumon

Salmone & Salmone

Salmón ahumado Benfumat Nature
Caviar de salmón Benfumat
Yogur griego
Hojas de hinojo
Aceite de girasol
1 vaina de vainilla
4 cucharadas de aceite de girasol

Calentar el aceite sin que llegue a hervir y poner el salmón de manera que quede bien sumergido durante 20 minutos. Sacar y escurrir con papel absorbente.

Cortar el salmón en lonchas de 0,5 cm de grosor y ponerlas en un plato alargado. Disponer sobre cada pieza de salmón una buena cucharada de caviar de salmón y aliñarlo con cuatro gotas de aceite de vainilla.
Verter el yogur en un biberón para decorar el plato con rayas finas. Encima, echar de nuevo aceite de vainilla. Como toque final, decorar cada montadito con una hoja de hinojo.
Aceite de vainilla: mezclar 1 vaina de vainilla con cuatro cucharadas de aceite de girasol.

Smoked salmon Benfumat Nature
Salmon caviar Benfumat
Greek yogurt
Fennel leaves
Sunflower oil
1 vanilla bean
4 tbsp of sunflower oil

Heat the oil without bringing to a boil, enough to submerge the salmon for 20 minutes. Remove and drain with absorbent paper towels.

Slice the salmon into 0.2 in. slices and place on an elongated plate. Place a spoonful of salmon caviar onto each slice of salmon and season with four drops of vanilla oil.
Squeeze yogurt through a baby bottle in order to decorate the plate with fine lines. Pour vanilla oil over the yogurt. For the final touch, decorate each slice with a small fennel leaf.
Vanilla oil: mix one vanilla bean with four tbsp of sunflower oil.

Räucherlachs Benfumat Nature
Lachskaviar Benfumat
Griechischer Jogurt
Fenchelzweige
Sonnenblumenöl
1 Vanilleschote
4 EL Sonnenblumenöl

Das Öl erhitzen, ohne dass es siedet, und den Lachs ganz eintauchen und 20 Minuten ziehen lassen. Herausnehmen und auf Küchenpapier abtropfen lassen.

Den Lachs in 0,5 cm dünne Scheiben schneiden und auf einen länglichen Teller legen. Auf jede Lachsscheibe einen gehäuften Löffel Lachskaviar geben und mit vier Tropfen Vanilleöl beträufeln.
Den Jogurt in eine Spritztüte füllen und den Teller mit feinen Streifen dekorieren. Auch über den Jogurt Vanilleöl träufeln. Zum Abschluss jedes Lachshäufchen mit einem Fenchelzweig garnieren.
Vanilleöl: eine Vanilleschote mit vier Esslöffeln Sonnenblumenöl vermischen.

Saumon fumé Benfumat Nature
Caviar de saumon Benfumat
Yaourt grec
Feuilles de fenouil
Huile de tournesol
1 gousse de vanille
4 c. à soupe d'huile de tournesol

Chauffer l'huile sans la faire bouillir et placer le saumon de sorte qu'il soit bien immergé durant 20 minutes. Le sortir et éponger l'huile avec du papier absorbant.

Préparer des darnes de saumon de 0,5 cm d'épaisseur et les poser dans un plat allongé. Disposer sur chaque darne de saumon une bonne cuillerée de caviar de saumon et l'assaisonner de quatre gouttes d'huile de vanille.
Verser le yaourt dans un biberon afin de décorer le plat de traits fins. Verser à nouveau de l'huile de vanille. Une touche finale : décorer chaque préparation de saumon d'une feuille de fenouil.
Huile de vanille : mélanger 1 gousse de vanille avec quatre cuillères à soupe d'huile de tournesol.

Salmone affumicato Benfumat Nature
Caviale di salmone Benfumat
Yogurt greco
Foglie di finocchio
Olio di girasole
1 baccello di vaniglia
4 cucchiai di olio di girasole

Riscaldare l'olio senza che arrivi a ebollizione e mettervi il salmone, in modo che sia ben sommerso, durante 20 minuti. Togliere e asciugare con carta da cucina.

Tagliare il salmone a tranci di mezzo cm di spessore e metterli in un piatto allungato. Su ogni pezzo di salmone disporre una buona cucchiaiata di caviale di salmone e irrorarlo con quattro gocce di olio di vaniglia.
Versare lo yogurt in un biberon per poter decorare il piatto con delle righe sottili.
Sullo yogurt versare un'altra volta olio di vaniglia. Come tocco finale, decorare ogni trancio di salmone con una piccola foglia di finocchio.
Olio di vaniglia: mescolare un baccello di vaniglia con quattro cucchiai di olio di girasole.

Drolma

Design: Josep Juanpere I Chef: Fermín Puig

Passeig de Gràcia 70 I 08007 Barcelona
Phone: +34 934 967 710
www.hotelmajestic.es
Subway: Passeig de Gràcia
Opening hours: Mon–Sat 1 pm to 3:30 pm, and 8:30 pm to 11 pm
Average price: € 125
Cuisine: Creative
Special features: Restaurant at the luxurious Hotel Majestic

Cigalas
con alcachofas

Prawns with Artichokes

Kaisergranat mit Artischocken

Écrevisses aux artichauts

Scampi coi carciofi

12 cigalas de 90–100 g
18 alcachofas
1 manzana golden
100 g de panceta ahumada
20 g de trufa de verano
150 g de pasta philo
50 g de mantequilla clarificada
Aceite de jengibre

Hacer unos crujientes de pasta philo a tres capas y pincelar con la mantequilla. Saltear las alcachofas una vez torneadas y laminadas.

Montar las alcachofas sobre los crujientes y reservar.
Pelar las cigalas y guardar las colas en el frigorífico.
Saltear la manzana en dados de mantequilla, sal, azúcar y pimienta.
Marcar las cigalas en una sartén y pincelarlas con aceite de jengibre.
Emplatado: Sobre los crujientes reservados, montar las cigalas, la manzana salteada, la panceta ahumada y añadir un poco de trufa de verano. Terminar con un aliño muy suave.

12 prawns (each about 3 1/2 oz)
18 artichokes
1 golden apple
3 1/2 oz of smoked bacon
1/2 oz of summer truffle
5 oz of philo pasta
1 1/2 oz of melted butter
Ginger oil

With triple-layers of philo pasta, make several biscuits and brush over with butter. Sauté the artichokes once cut and sliced.

Place artichokes over the biscuits and set aside.
Peel the prawns and keep the tails inside the refrigerator.
Sauté the apple in cubes of butter, salt, sugar and pepper.
Sauté the prawns inside a pan and brush over with ginger oil.
To serve: On the triple-layers of philo-pasta set aside, place the prawns, sauteed apple, smoked bacon and add summer truffle. Top with a light seasoning.

12 Kaisergranate (je 90–110 g)
18 Artischocken
1 Apfel (Golden Delicious)
100 g durchwachsener Räucherspeck
20 g Sommertrüffel
150 g Philoteig
50 g zerlassene Butter
Ingweröl

Aus drei Lagen Philoteig knusprige Plätzchen bereiten und mit Butter bestreichen. Die geputzten Artischocken in Scheiben schneiden und sautieren.

Dann auf die knusprigen Teigblätter legen und beiseite stellen.
Die Kaisergranate pellen und die Schwänze im Kühlschrank aufbewahren.
Den Apfel in Würfel schneiden und in Butter mit Zucker, Salz und Pfeffer anbräunen.
In einer Pfanne die Kaisergranate anbraten und mit Ingweröl bepinseln.
Serviervorschlag: Die Kaisergranate auf die vorbereiteten Teigblätter mit den Artischocken legen, darüber die sautierten Apfelwürfel, den Räucherspeck und die Sommertrüffeln geben. Sehr mild würzen.

---

12 écrevisses de 90–100 g
18 artichauts
1 pomme golden
100 g de pancetta fumée
20 g de truffe d'été
150 g de pâte philo
50 g de beurre clarifié
Huile de gingembre

Réaliser des croissants de pâte philo à trois couches et badigeonner de beurre. Faire sauter les artichauts une fois nettoyés et émincés.

Disposer les artichauts sur les croissants et réserver.
Décortiquer les écrevisses et conserver les queues au réfrigérateur.
Faire sauter la pomme en dés dans le beurre, le sel, le sucre et le poivre.
Braiser les écrevisses à la poêle et les enduire d'huile de gingembre.
Présentation : Sur les croissants réservés, monter les écrevisses, la pomme sautée, la pancetta fumée et émincé avec la truffe d'été. Terminer en assaisonnant très légèrement.

---

12 scampi da 90–100 g
18 carciofi
1 mela golden
100 g di pancetta affumicata
20 g di tartufo nero
150 g di pasta filo
50 g di burro schiarito
Olio di zenzero

Fare dei croccanti di pasta filo a tre strati e spennellarli con il burro. Rosolare i carciofi dopo averli puliti e tagliati a lamelle.

Sistemare i carciofi sui croccanti e mettere da parte.
Pelare gli scampi e conservare le code in frigorifero.
Saltare i dadini di mela nel burro, con sale, zucchero e pepe.
Passare gli scampi in padella e spennellarli con olio di zenzero.
Presentazione: Collocare gli scampi sui croccanti messi da parte, poi la mela, la pancetta affumicata e tartufo nero. Terminare con un condimento molto leggero.

Espai Sucre

Design: Alfons Tost | Chefs: Xano Saguer, Jordi Butron,
Santi Rebes

Carrer de la Princesa 53 | 08003 Barcelona
Phone: +34 932 681 630
www.espaisucre.com
Subway: Jaume I, Arc de Triomf
Opening hours: Tue–Thu 9 pm to 11:30 pm, Fri and Sat 8:30 pm to midnight
Average price: 3 desserts menu: € 25, 5 desserts menu: € 33, varied menu: € 45
Cuisine: Creative, desserts restaurant
Special features: Houses a school of desserts

Leche picante
con manzana y kefir

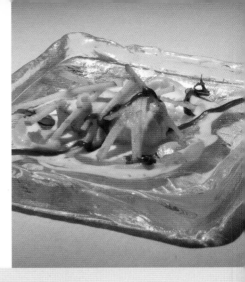

Spicy Milk with Apple and Kefir

Scharfe Milch mit Apfel und Kefir

Lait piquant avec pomme et kéfir

Latte piccante con mela e kefir

Leche picante: 1,5 l de leche, 75 g de azúcar, pimienta negra, jengibre y agar-agar. Hervir todos los ingredientes, pasar la mezcla por la batidora y verter en un molde de 2 cm de altura. Reservar en frío.
Crema de limón: 25 g de corteza de limón. 270 ml de zumo de limón, 9 huevos, 20 g de mantequilla, 20 g de maizena y 150 g de azúcar. Remover todos los ingredientes constantemente en un recipiente al baño maría hasta que adquieran consistencia.
Caramelo a la pimienta negra: 125 g de glucosa, 125 g de azúcar y pimienta en polvo. Poner la glucosa y el azúcar al fuego hasta que la mezcla empieza a coger color. Retirar del fuego y añadir la pimienta. Echar sobre una hoja de silicona y poner otra hoja encima; con un rodillo de pastelería extender hasta obtener una fina lámina de caramelo.
Emplatado: Sobre dos pellizcos de mermelada de naranja colocar dos pequeños cuadrados de leche picante en un plato, y bañarlos con kéfir. Encima, añadir una juliana de manzana verde y cuatro pedacitos del cristal de caramelo de pimienta. Alrededor dibujar unas cuantas líneas de crema de limón y unas hojas de rúcula selvática. Finalmente, hacer una línea transversal de jarabe de toffee y rallar un poco de piel de lima.

Spicy milk: 1,5 l of milk, 2 1/2 oz of sugar, black pepper, ginger and agar-agar. Boil the ingredients, mix inside a blender and pour 7/10 into a mold. Refrigerate.
Lemon custard: 1 oz of lemon rind, 270 ml of lemon juice, 9 eggs, 1/2 oz of butter, 1/2 oz of cornstarch and 5 oz of sugar. Stir the ingredients continuously inside a double-boiler until thick.
Black Peppered Caramel: 4 oz of glucose, 4 oz of sugar and powdered pepper. Place the glucose and sugar over the fire until it acquires color. Remove from the heat and add the pepper. Serve onto a silicone sheet and cover with another sheet; flatten and stretch with a rolling pin to obtain a thin layer of caramel.
To serve: Place two small cubes of spicy milk on top of two spoonfuls of orange marmalade on a plate and cover with kefir. Lay apple strips on top, along with four small chunks of peppered caramel. Adorn the plate with strokes of lemon custard and a few leaves of wild rucula. Finally, make a transversal line with toffee sirup and sprinkle with grated lime.

Scharfe Milch: 1,5 l Milch, 75 g Zucker, schwarzer Pfeffer, Ingwer, Agar-Agar. Alle Zutaten zusammen kochen, mit dem Rührstab mixen und in eine Form mit 2 cm hohem Rand schütten. Kalt stellen.
Zitronencreme: 25 g Zitronenschale, 270 ml Zitronensaft, 9 Eier, 20 g Butter, 20 g Mondamin und 150 g Zucker. Alle Zutaten unter Rühren im Wasserbad erhitzen, bis die Masse fest wird.
Karamell mit schwarzem Pfeffer: 125 g Traubenzucker, 125 g Zucker und schwarzer Pfeffer. Den Zucker erhitzen, bis er beginnt braun zu werden. Vom Feuer nehmen und den Pfeffer dazugeben. Auf einer Folie ausbreiten, eine andere Folie darüberlegen und mit dem Nudelholz ausrollen, bis eine feine Karamellschicht entsteht.
Serviervorschlag: Auf jeden Teller je zwei kleine Häufchen Orangenmarmelade geben, zwei kleine Würfel scharfe Milch darauf setzen und Kefir darum gießen. Mit einem Streifen grünem Apfel und vier Karamellsplittern bekrönen. Drumherum einige Linien Zitronencreme und ein paar wilde Ruccolablätter verteilen. Abschließend eine schräge Linie Toffee–Sirup ziehen und etwas Zitronenschale darüberreiben.

Lait piquant : 1,5 l de lait, 75 g de sucre, poivre noir, gingembre et agar-agar. Faire bouillir tous les ingrédients, passer le mélange au mixer et verser dans un moule de 2 cm de haut. Réserver au frais.
Crème de citron : 25 g de zest de citron, 270 ml de jus de citron, 9 œufs, 20 g de beurre, 20 g de maïzena et 150 g de sucre. Mélanger tous les ingrédients constamment dans un récipient au bain-marie jusqu'à obtention de la consistance.
Caramel au poivre noir : 125 g de glucose, 125 g de sucre et poivre moulu. Mettre le glucose et le sucre sur le feu jusqu'à coloration. Retirer du feu et ajouter le poivre. Verser sur une feuille de silicone et recouvrir d'une seconde feuille puis étirer avec un rouleau afin d'obtenir une fine couche de caramel.
Présentation : Sur deux pincées de confiture d'orange, disposer deux petits carré de lait piquant dans un plat et les baigner de kéfir. Dessus, ajouter une julienne de pomme verte et quatre petits morceaux de caramel au poivre noir. Autour, dessiner quelques lignes de crème de citron et quelques feuilles de roquette sauvage. Finalement, réaliser une transversale de sirop de toffee et râper un peu de zeste de citron vert.

Latte piccante: 1,5 l di latte, 75 g di zucchero, pepe nero, zenzero e agar-agar. Bollire tutti gli ingredienti, passare il composto nel frullatore e versare in uno stampo di 2 cm d'altezza. Mettere in frigo.
Crema di limone: 25 g di scorza di limone, 270 ml di succo di limone, 9 uova, 20 g de burro, 20 g di maizena e 150 g di zucchero. Mescolare tutti gli ingredienti senza interruzione in un recipiente a bagno maria finchè la crema prende consistenza.
Caramello al pepe nero: 125 g di glucosio, 125 g di zucchero e pepe in polvere. Mettere il glucosio e lo zucchero sul fuoco finchè cominciano a prendere colore. Ritirare dal fuoco e aggiungere il pepe. Versare su un foglio di silicone e mettere un altro foglio sopra; con un matterello tirare fino ad ottenere una lamina sottile di caramello.
Presentazione: In un piatto collocare su due pizzichi di marmellata d'arancia due piccoli quadrati di latte piccante e bagnarli di kefir. Aggiungere sopra una julienne di mela verde e quattro pezzetti di caramello al pepe. Tutt'intorno disegnare le linee di crema di limone e delle foglie di rucola selvatica. Quindi fare una linea trasversale di sciroppo di toffee e grattugiare un poco di pelle di lime.

Freud b'ART

Design: Oliver Bals | Chef: Gianni Fusco

Baixada de Sant Miquel 4 | 08002 Barcelona
Phone: +34 933 186 629
www.freudbart.com   info@freudbart.com
Subway: Jaume I, Liceu
Opening hours: Tue–Fri 8:30 pm to 11 pm, Sat 1:30 pm to 4 pm and 8:30 pm to midnight
Average price: € 22
Cuisine: Mediterranean
Special features: Houses an art gallery

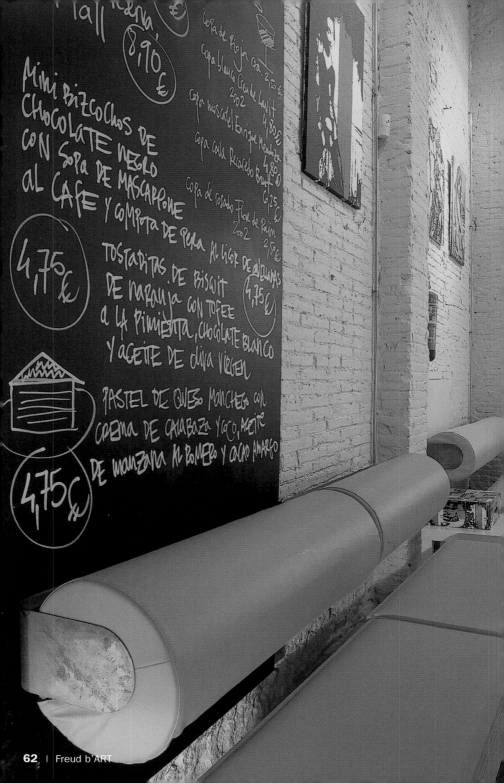

Chupito
de aguacate y langostinos

Avocado and Prawn Shot

Avocadococktail an Langostinos

« Chupito » d'avocat et de langoustines

"Sobetto" di avocado e gamberoni

1 aguacate maduro
1 cucharada de mayonesa
1 nuez de mantequilla
50 ml de crema de leche (35%)
Sal y pimienta
Zumo de limón (al gusto)
4 langostinos (dos por chupito)
1 puerro pequeño
Aceite de oliva virgen
2 vainas de vainilla

Introducir las vainas de vainilla en aceite de oliva caliente sin que llegue al punto de ebullición durante media hora.

Pelar los langostinos y reservar las cabezas. Saltear las colas con la mantequilla.
Poner agua en un cazo y añadir el puerro y las cabezas; hervir durante media hora aproximadamente hasta obtener un caldo.
En un bol, disponer el aguacate pelado, la mayonesa, el zumo de limón y la nata y salpimentar. Pasar por la batidora. Añadir a esta mezcla el caldo de langostinos hasta obtener la consistencia deseada.
Verter la crema resultante en vasos de chupito, añadir los langostinos tibios y salsear con el aceite de vainilla.

1 ripe avocado
1 tbsp of mayonnaise
1 hazel-nut sized drop of butter
50 ml cooking cream (35%)
Salt and pepper
Lemon juice (to taste)
4 prawns (two per shot)
1 small leek
Virgin olive oil
2 vanilla beans

Introduce the vanilla beans in hot olive oil without bringing to boil for half an hour.

Peel the prawns and save the heads.
Sauté the tails in butter.
Place water in a pot and boil the leek and prawn heads for approximately half an hour until obtaining a stock.
In a bowl, place the peeled avocado, mayonnaise, lemon juice and cream and season with salt and pepper. Mix with a blender. Add the prawn stock to this mix until obtaining the desired consistency.
Pour into shot glasses, adding the warm prawns and seasoning with vanilla oil.

1 reife Avocado
1 EL Mayonnaise
1 Butterflocke
50 ml Sahne (35%)
Salz und Pfeffer
Zitronensaft (nach Geschmack)
4 Langostinos (zwei pro Cocktail)
1 kleine Lauchstange
Kaltgepresstes Olivenöl
2 Vanilleschoten

Die Vanilleschoten eine halbe Stunde in heißes,
nicht siedendes Olivenöl legen.

Die Langostinos pellen und die Köpfe aufheben.
Die Schwänze in Butter bräunen.
In einer Kasserole Wasser erhitzen, den Lauch
und die Langostinoköpfe hineingeben und eine
gute halbe Stunde kochen, um eine Brühe zu
bereiten.
Die geschälte Avocado, Mayonnaise, Zitronensaft und Sahne in eine Schüssel geben und mit
dem Rührstab mixen, salzen und pfeffern.
Soviel Langostinenbrühe dazugeben, bis die ge-
wünschte Konsistenz erreicht ist.
Die Creme in Schnapsgläser füllen, die lau-
warmen Langostinos dazulegen und mit Vanilleöl beträufeln.

1 avocat mûr
1 c. à soupe de mayonnaise
1 noix de beurre
50 ml de crème liquide (35%)
Sel et poivre
Jus de citron (selon les goûts)
4 langoustines (deux par verre à goutte)
1 petit poireau
Huile d'olive vierge
2 gousses de vanille

Introduire les gousses de vanille dans l'huile
d'olive chaude sans atteindre l'ébullition durant
une demi heure.

Décortiquer les langoustines et réserver les têtes.
Faire sauter les queues dans le beurre.
Mettre l'eau dans une casserole et ajouter le
poireau avec les têtes puis faire bouillir durant
une demi heure environ pour obtenir un bouillon.
Dans un bol, disposer l'avocat pelé, la mayonnaise, le jus de citron et la crème puis assaisonner de sel et de poivre. Passer au mixer.
Ajouter au mélange le bouillon de langoustine
pour obtenir la consistance voulue.
Verser la crème dans des verres à goutte (« chupito »), ajouter les langoustines tièdes et saucer
avec l'huile de vanille.

1 avocado maturo
1 cucchiaio di maionese
1 noce di burro
50 ml di crema di latte (35%)
Sale e pepe
Succo di limone (al gusto)
4 gamberoni (due per sorbetto)
1 porro piccolo
Olio di oliva extra vergine
2 baccelli di vaniglia

Introdurre i baccelli di vaniglia nell'olio d'oliva
caldo senza che arrivi al punto di bollore durante mezz'ora.

Pelare i gamberoni e mettere da parte le teste.
Saltare le code in padella con un pó di burro.
Mettere dell'acqua in un tegame e aggiungere il
porro e le teste; bollire mezz'ora circa per ottenere un brodo.
Collocare in una terrina l'avocado pelato, la
maionese, il succo di limone e la panna e condire il tutto per poi passarlo nel frullatore. Aggiungere a questo composto il brodo di gamberoni fino ad ottenere la consistenza desiderata.
Versare la crema ottenuta in bicchieri da sorbetto, aggiungere i gamberoni tiepidi e condire con
l'olio alla vaniglia.

Little Italy

Design: Camila Hamm, Alberto Esquerdo |
Chef: Vicente Vázquez

Carrer del Rec 30 | 08003 Barcelona
Phone: +34 933 197 973
www.restaurantlittleitaly.com
Subway: Jaume I
Opening hours: Everyday 1 pm to 4 pm, Sat–Sun 9 pm to midnight, too
Average price: € 25
Cuisine: Italian
Special features: Live music

Selección

de la carta

Menu Selection

Auswahl à la carte

Sélection à la carte

Scelta dal menù

Entrantes:
Surtido de ensaladas con jamón de pato y viru-
tas de foie con vinagreta de frambuesa
Ensalada de espinacas y tomate braseado con
láminas de parmesano al aceite de oliva virgen
Tartar de tomate y carabineros con guacamole a
la vinagreta de cítricos

Pastas y arroz:
Risotto de alcachofas y chipirones al azafrán
Láminas de pasta con verduras asadas y salsa
romesco
Panzerotti e bacalao con sofrito mediterráneo y
tapenada de olivas negras

Pescados:
Lomo de bacalao con mermelada de tomate del
Montseny y albahaca crujiente

Caballa confitada en aceite de oliva con lentejas
y texturas de puerros
Carpaccio de gambas con aceite de anchoas
Carnes:
Magret de pato confitado con higos al aroma de
Calvados
Solomillo de ternera con escalope de hígado de
pato al oporto
Carpaccio de buey al parmesano con aceite de
nueces de Macadamia

Postres:
Canelón de plátano y dátiles con sorbete de
mango y natilla de coco
Tarta de manzanas al romero, helado de arroz
con leche y teja de miel
Frutas frescas en gelatina suave de clementi-
nas al cava

Starters:
Assortment of salads with duck meat and grated foie with raspberry vinagrette
Spinach and grilled tomato salad with parmesan
shavings and virgin olive oil
Tomato tartar and shrimp with guacamole and
citric vinaigrette

Pastas and rice:
Artichoke and baby squid saffron risotto
Laminas of pasta with grilled vegetables and
romesco sauce
Panzerotti and codfish with mediterranean sauté
and black olives

Fish:
Loin of codfish with tomato marmalade from
Montseny and crispy basil

Crystallized mackerel in olive oil with lentils and
leek
Prawn carpaccio with anchovy oil

Meat:
Caramelized duck magret with Calvados flavored
figs
Veal steak with duck liver cutlet cooked in Port
wine
Ox carpaccio with parmesan with Macadamia
nut oil

Desserts:
Banana and dates with mango sorbet and co-
conut custard
Rosemary apple cake, rice ice cream with milk
and honey
Fresh fruit in soft champagne Clementine gelatine

Vorspeisen:
Salatteller mit Entenschinken, Flocken aus Paté de Foie und Himbeervinaigrette
Salat aus Spinatblättern und gegrillter Tomate mit Parmesanscheiben und kaltgepresstem Olivenöl
Tartar aus Tomate und Riesengarnelen mit Guacamole-Soße und Zitrusvinaigrette

Reis- und Nudelgerichte:
Risotto mit Artischocken und Babytintenfischen in Safran
Nudelscheiben mit gegrilltem Gemüse und Romesco-Soße
Panzerotti und Stockfisch in Mittelmeersofrito mit schwarzer Olivenpaste

Fischgerichte:
Stockfischrücken mit Tomatenmarmelade vom Montseny und knusprigem Basilikum

In Olivenöl eingemachte Makrele mit Linsen und Lauch
Garnelencarpaccio und Sardellenöl

Fleischgerichte:
Eingemachte Entenbrust an Feigen mit Calvadosaroma
Kalbsmedaillon mit Entenleberschnitzel in Portwein
Ochsencarpaccio mit Parmesan und Makadamianüssen

Desserts:
Bananen-Dattel-Rolle mit Mangosorbet und Kokossahnecreme
Apfeltorte mit Rosmarin, Milchreiseis und Honigziegel
Frisches Obst in milder Götterspeise aus Klementinen mit Sekt

---

Entrées :
Assiette de salade aux magrets de canard et copeaux de foie au vinaigre de framboise
Salade d'épinards et de tomates braisées parsemée de lamelles de parmesan à l'huile d'olive vierge
Tartare de tomate et crevettes impériales avec guacamole à la vinaigrette d'agrumes

Pâtes et riz:
Risotto d'artichauts et de petits calmars au safran
Feuilles de pâtes et légumes sautés à la sauce romesco
Panzerotti et morue avec sofrito méditerranéen et tapenade d'olives noires

Poissons :
Filets de morue à la confiture de tomate de Montseny et basilic croquant

Maquereau confit dans l'huile d'olive avec lentilles et textures de poireaux
Carpaccio de crevettes à l'huile d'anchois.

Viandes :
Magret de canard confit et figues aux arômes de Calvados
Aloyau de veau et escalope de foie de canard au porto
Carpaccio de bœuf au parmesan à l'huile de noix de macadamia

Desserts :
Cannellonis de bananes et dattes avec sorbet de mangue et crème de coco
Tarte aux pommes au romarin, glace de riz au lait et tuile de miel
Fruits frais en gélatine sucrée de clémentines au champagne

Antipasti:
Varietà di insalate con prosciutto d'anatra e trucioli di foie con vinagrette di lamponi
Insalata di spinaci e pomodori arrostiti con scaglie di parmigiano all'olio extra vergine d'oliva
Tartara di pomodori e gamberi rossi con guacamole alla vinagrette di agrumi

Pasta e riso:
Risotto di calamari allo zafferano
Sfoglie di pasta con verdure alla griglia e salsa rimesco
Panzerotti e baccalà con soffritto mediterraneo e olive nere

Pesce:
Lombo di baccalà con marmellata di pomodoro del Montseny e basilico croccante

Sgombro sciroppato in olio d'oliva con lenticchie e intrecci di porri
Carpaccio di gamberi con olio d'acciughe

Carne:
Magret d'anatra sciroppato con fichi all'aroma di Calvados
Filetto di vitello con scaloppina di fegato d'oca al Porto
Carpaccio di manzo con olio di noci di Macadamia

Dolci:
Cannellone di banana e datteri con sorbetto di mango e crema di cocco
Torta di mele al rosmarino, gelato di riso con latte e tegola di mele
Frutta fresca in gelatina dolce di clementine allo spumante

Lupino Lounge Restaurant

Design: Xavier Franquesa, Ellen Rapelius I Chef: Pol Garcia

Carrer del Carme 33 I 08001 Barcelona
Phone: +34 934 123 697 I www.stnex.com
Subway: Liceu
Opening hours: Everyday 1:30 pm to 4 pm, and 9 pm to 1 am
Average price: € 28 – € 30
Cuisine: Mediterranean-Basque-Catalan
Special features: Ultra trendy, disc-jockeys

Rape asado
con jugo de ceps

Monkfish with Ceps Sauce

Gegrillter Seeteufel mit Steinpilzsoße

Lotte grillée au jus de ceps

Coda di rospo arrosto con sugo
di porcini

4 raciones de rape
1 bróculi
300 g de mantequilla
50 g de polvo de ceps
100 ml de agua de ceps
200 ml de aceite de ceps
1 yuca

Rebozar el rape con el polvo de ceps, salpimentar y poner en la parrilla hasta que esté dorado. Por otro lado, cocer el bróculi hasta que quede muy blando (15 minutos aproximadamente), escurrir el agua, salpimentar y pasar por la batidora junto con la mantequilla. Reservar.

Calentar el agua de ceps, una vez caliente pasar por la batidora añadiendo poco a poco el aceite de ceps y montando como si de una mayonesa se tratara.
Cortar la yuca en láminas finas –a ser posible utilizar un cortafiambres– y freírla en abundante aceite de girasol muy caliente. Escurrir.
Emplatado: Disponer en un plato tres cucharadas de puré de bróculi en forma de círculo; hacer unas aspas sobre el puré con la emulsión de ceps y colocar el rape desespinado. Cubrir con los chips de yuca.

4 portions of monkfish
1 broccoli
10 1/2 oz of butter
1 1/2 oz of ceps powder
100 ml of ceps water
200 ml of ceps oil
1 yuca

Dip the monkfish in the ceps powder, season with salt and pepper and place on the grill until golden.
Separately, boil the broccoli until tender (approximately 15 minutes), strain, add salt and

pepper, and mix in a blender with butter. Set aside.
Heat the ceps water, and once hot, place inside a blender and little by little add the ceps oil as if making mayonnaise.
Cut the yuca into fine slices—if possible use a slicing machine—and fry in abundant sunflower oil on high heat. Drain.
To serve: Place three spoonfuls of broccoli purée in a circular form; with the ceps emulsion make cross-shaped strokes over the purée and place the boned monkfish. Cover with yuca chips.

4 Portionen Seeteufel
1 Broccoli
300 g Butter
50 g Steinpilzpulver
100 ml Steinpilzsud
200 ml Steinpilzöl
1 Yucca

Den Seeteufel in Steinpilzpulver wenden, salzen und pfeffern und goldbraun grillen.
Den Broccoli sehr weich kochen (etwa 15 Minuten), das Wasser abgießen, salzen und pfeffern, Butter zugeben und mit dem Mixstab pürieren. Beiseite stellen.

Den Steinpilzsud erhitzen und mit einem Rührgerät nach und nach wie eine Mayonnaise mit dem Steinpilzöl vermengen.
Die Yucca in feine Scheiben schneiden – möglichst mit einer Wurstschneidemaschine – und in reichlich sehr heißem Sonnenblumenöl fritieren. Abtropfen lassen.
Serviervorschlag: Drei Esslöffel Broccolipüree auf einem Teller ringförmig anordnen, darüber mit der Steinpilzsoße Kreuze zeichnen und das entgrätete Seeteufelfleisch auflegen. Dann mit den Yuccachips bedecken.

4 parts de lotte
1 brocoli
300 g de beurre
50 g de poudre de ceps
100 ml de jus de ceps
200 ml d'huile de ceps
1 yucca

Paner la lotte dans la poudre de ceps, assaisonner de sel et de poivre et passer au grill pour colorer d'une teinte dorée.
D'autre part, cuire le brocoli pour le ramollir complètement (15 minutes environ), égoutter,

assaisonner de sel et de poivre puis passer au mixer avec le beurre. Réserver.
Chauffer le jus de ceps et, une fois chaud, le passer au mixer en ajoutant peu à peu l'huile de ceps et monter comme pour une mayonnaise.
Couper le yucca en fines tranches (si possible à la trancheuse, et frire dans de l'huile de tournesol abondante et très chaude. Égoutter.
Présentation : Disposer dans un plat trois cuillères de purée de brocoli en forme de cercle. Dessiner des ailes sur la purée avec l'émulsion de ceps et disposer la lotte filetée. Couvrir des chips de yucca.

4 razioni di coda di rospo
1 broccolo
300 g di burro
50 g di polvere di funghi porcini
100 ml di acqua di porcini
200 ml di olio di porcini
1 yucca

Passare la coda di rospo nella polvere di porcini, salare e disporre sulla griglia finchè risulta dorato.
A parte cuocere il broccolo finchè diventa molto tenero (15 minuti circa), scolarlo, salarlo e frullarlo col burro. Mettere da parte.

Riscaldare l'acqua di porcini, poi frullarla aggiungendo poco alla volta l'olio di porcini per montarla come se fosse una maionese.
Tagliare la yucca a fettine sottili (se è possibile usare l'affettatrice) e friggerla in abbondante olio di girasole bollente. Sgocciolare.
Presentazione: Disporre in un piatto tre cucchiaiate di purè di broccoli in forma circolare; disegnare con l'emulsione di porcini delle croci e collocare la coda di rospo diliscata. Coprire con le patatine di yucca.

Moo

Design: Sandra Tarruella, Isabel López |
Chef: Felip Llufriu

Carrer Rosselló 265 | 08007 Barcelona
Phone: +34 934 454 000
www.hotelomm.es
Subway: Diagonal
Opening hours: Everyday from 1:30 pm to 4 pm, and from 8:30 pm to 11 pm
Average price: € 60
Cuisine: Creative
Special features: Great selection of wines

Parmentier
de calamares

Squid Parmentier

Parmentier mit Tintenfischen

Parmentier de calmars

Parmentier di calamari

400 g de calamares
400 g de chipirones
200 g de patatas
50 g de aceite
50 g de crema de leche
20 g de pimienta roja
20 g de sal

Hacer un puré de patata con la crema de leche y aceite. Reservar.

Limpiar los calamares y cortarlos en tiras de 0,5 cm aproximadamente. Aliñarlos con sal, pimienta roja y disponerlos alineados unos junto a otros para congelar en una sola pieza. Con los restos sobrantes hacer un caldo.
Limpiar y saltear los chipirones.
Emplatado: Poner dos cucharadas de puré caliente; cubrir con rodajas de calamar muy finas cortadas con un cortafiambres. Pasar por la salamandra. Añadir los chipirones y salsear con una emulsión de caldo de calamar.

14 oz of squid
14 oz of baby squid
7 oz of potato
1 1/2 oz of oil
1 1/2 oz of cooking cream
1/2 oz of red pepper
1/2 oz of salt

Make a potato purée with cream and oil. Set aside.

Wash the squid and slice in strips of approximately 1/2 in. Season with salt, red pepper and align together to freeze in one piece. Make a stock with the leftovers.
Wash and sauté the baby squid.
To serve: Top two spoonfuls of hot purée with finely sliced squid rings. Grill in the oven. Add baby squid and season with stock.

400 g Tintenfische (Kalmare)
400 g Babytintenfische
200 g Kartoffeln
50 g Öl
50 g Sahne
20 g roter Pfeffer
20 g Salz

Ein Kartoffelpüree bereiten und mit Sahne und
Öl verfeinern. Beiseite stellen.

Die Tintenfische putzen und in etwa 0,5 cm
dicke Ringe schneiden. Mit Salz und rotem Pfeffer würzen, dicht an dicht legen und in einem
Stück einfrieren. Aus den Resten eine Brühe
bereiten.
Die Babytintenfische putzen und anbraten.
Serviervorschlag: Zwei Esslöffel warmes Püree
mit sehr fein geschnittenen Tintenfischscheiben
belegen. Überbacken. Die Babytintenfische
dazugeben und mit eingedickter Tintenfisch-
brühe als Soße servieren.

400 g de calmars
400 g de petits calmars
200 g de pommes de terre
50 g d'huile
50 g de crème liquide
20 g de poivre rouge
20 g de sel

Réaliser une purée de pommes de terre avec la
crème liquide et l'huile. Réserver.

Laver les calmars et les couper en lanières de
0,5 cm environ. Assaisonner avec la sel, le poivre rouge et les disposer les uns à côté des autres pour les congeler d'une seule pièce. Avec
les restes, préparer un bouillon.
Laver et faire sauter les petits calmars.
Présentation : Disposer deux cuillères de purée
chaude, couvrir de tranches de calmars finement émincées à la trancheuse. Passer à la sa-
lamandre ou au grill. Ajouter les petits calmars
et saucer de l'émulsion de bouillon de calmar.

400 g di calamari
400 g di calamaretti
200 g di patate
50 g di olio
50 g di crema di latte
20 g di pepe rosso
20 g di sale

Fare un purè di patate con la crema di latte e l'o-
lio. Mettere da parte.

Pulire i calamari e tagliarli in strisce di mezzo
centimetro circa. Condirli con la sale, il pepe
rosso e disporli allineati uno vicino all'altro per
congelarli in un unico pezzo. Con i resti preparare un brodo.
Pulire a rosolare i calamaretti.
Presentazione: Mettere due cucchiaiate di purè
caldo, coprire con anelli di calamari molto sottili tagliati con un'affettatrice. Riscaldare. Aggiungere i calamaretti e condire con un'emulsione di
brodo di calamari.

Neri H&R

Design: Cristina Gabás | Chef: Manuel Marín

Carrer de Sant Sever 5 | 08002 Barcelona
Phone: +34 933 040 655
www.hotelneri.com
Subway: Liceu, Jaime I
Opening hours: Everyday 1:30 pm to 3:30 pm, and 8:30 pm to 11 pm
Average price: € 40 – € 50
Cuisine: Aromatic Mediterranean
Special features: Housed in a remodeled Gothic palace

Huevo escalfado

con ceps y salsa de foie

Poached Egg with Ceps and Foie Sauce

Pochierte Eier mit Steinpilzen und Paté-de-Foie-Soße

Œufs pochés aux ceps et sauce au foie

Uovo affogato con porcini e salsa di foie

---

4 huevos
200 g de ceps frescos
10 ml aceite de trufa
200 g de foie mi-cuit
Crema de leche
5 g trufa
Sal maldon
Sal y pimienta

Extender sobre la mesa un trozo de papel transparente tamaño folio y pintar la cara superior con aceite de trufa. Abrir un huevo entero en el centro vigilando que no se rompa. Salar y hacer un paquetito anudando los cuatro extremos.

Poner agua a hervir e introducirlo cuando el agua haya llegado al punto de ebullición; hervir durante 4 minutos exactamente. Retirar el papel transparente.
Por otro lado, saltear los ceps con un poco de aceite y salpimentar. Reservar.
Hacer una salsa con el foie, la crema de leche, sal y pimienta; triturar hasta que quede bien homogénea.
Emplatado: Disponer los ceps en el centro del plato, colocar encima el huevo escalfado, salsear el huevo y los ceps con la salsa de foie y terminar con unas láminas de trufa y un poco de sal maldon.

---

4 eggs
7 oz of fresh ceps
10 ml of truffle oil
7 oz of foie "mi-cuit"
Cream of milk
0.17 oz of truffle
Maldon salt
Salt and pepper

Extend an A4 size of plastic wrap and brush over with truffle oil. Crack open one egg, making sure it does not break. Add salt and make a small

package by tying the four corners together. Place in boiling water for exactly 4 minutes. Remove the plastic wrap.
Separately, sauté the ceps with a bit of oil and season with salt and pepper. Set aside.
Make a sauce with the foie, cream, salt and pepper; blend until smooth.
To serve: Place the ceps in the center of a plate and on top, the poached egg, seasoning with the foie sauce, a few slivers of truffle and a bit of Maldon salt.

4 Eier
200 g frische Steinpilze
10 ml Trüffelöl
200 g Paté de Foie „mi-cuit" (Leberpastete)
Sahne
5 g Trüffeln
Maldonsalz
Salz und Pfeffer

Ein Stück Küchenfolie (DIN A4) mit Trüffelöl bepinseln. Über der Mitte des Blattes ein Ei aufschlagen, ohne das Dotter zu verletzen. Das Ei salzen und das Blatt an den vier Ecken hochnehmen und zusammenknoten. Das Päckchen in kochendes Wasser tauchen und das Ei genau vier Minuten kochen. Das Papier entfernen. Die Steinpilze in etwas Öl sautieren, salzen und pfeffern. Beiseite stellen. Leberpastete, Sahne, Salz und Pfeffer solange schlagen, bis eine glatte Soße entsteht. Serviervorschlag: Steinpilze in die Mitte des Tellers legen, das Ei darüber, dann alles mit der Soße begießen und mit einigen Trüffelscheibchen und etwas Maldonsalz bekrönen.

4 œufs
200 g de ceps frais
10 ml d'huile de truffe
200 g de foie mi-cuit
Crème liquide
5 g de truffe
Sel maldon
Sel et poivre

Étendre sur le plan de travail une feuille de papier transparent et badigeonner la face supérieure d'huile de truffe. Casser un œuf entier en son centre en s'assurant de ne pas le briser. Saler et réaliser un petit paquet en nouant les quatre extrémités. Faire bouillir l'eau et introduire le paquet à ébullition. Laisser bouillir durant 4 minutes exactement. Retirer le papier transparent. Par ailleurs, faire sauter les ceps dans d'un peu d'huile, saler et poivrer. Réserver. Préparer une sauce avec le foie, la crème liquide, le sel et le poivre. Bien homogénéiser. Présentation : Disposer les ceps au centre du plat, les couvrir de l'œuf poché, saucer le tout avec la sauce de foie et couronner de lamelles de truffe et d'un peu de sel maldon.

4 uova
200 g di porcini freschi
10 ml olio al tartufo
200 g di foie "mi-cuit"
Crema di latte
5 g di tartufo
Sale maldon
Sale e pepe

Stendere sul tavolo un pezzo di carta trasparente della dimensione di un foglio e spennellare la superficie con olio al tartufo. Aprire un uovo intero nel centro facendo attenzione che non si rompa. Salare e fare un pacchettino annodando le quattro estremità. Far bollire l'acqua e introdurlo quando l'acqua è arrivata al bollore; bollire esattamente 4 minuti. Togliere la carta trasparente. A parte rosolare i porcini con un po' d'olio e salare. Riservare. Fare una salsa col foie, la crema di latte, sale e pepe; triturare finché risulta omogenea. Presentazione: Disporre i porcini nel centro del piatto, collocare sopra l'uovo affogato, condire con la salsa di foie e terminare con delle scaglie di tartufo e un poco di sale maldon.

Noti Restaurant & Goodbar

Design: Francesc Pons | Chef: George Pierre

Carrer Roger de Llúria 35-37 | 08009 Barcelona
Phone: +34 933 426 673
www: noti-universal.com
Subway: Passeig de Gràcia, Urquinaona
Opening hours: Mon–Fri 1:30 pm to 4 pm, and 8:30 pm to midnight.
Sat 8:30 pm to midnight. Goodbar opens Mon–Sat 8 pm to 2:30 am
Average price: € 45 – € 50
Cuisine: Creative
Special features: Great design, glamourous clientelle

Rape a la plancha
con vinagreta de tomate

Grilled Monkfish with Tomato Vinaigrette

Gebratener Seeteufel mit Tomatenvinaigrette

Lotte braisée à la vinaigrette de tomate

Coda di rospo alla griglia con vinagrette di pomodoro

500 g de rape
12 espárragos verdes
8 cebolletas
1 limón
100 ml de aceite de oliva
1 tomate maduro
2 ramitas de romero

Confitar las cebolletas en aceite de oliva y escaldar los espárragos. Reservar.
Cortar en trozos pequeños el rape y pasarlo por la plancha hasta el punto de cocción que se desee.

Marcar los espárragos y las cebolletas a la plancha. Reservar.
Emplatado: Colocar el rape bien caliente sobre un lecho de espárragos y cebolletas, y aliñar con la vinagreta.
Vinagreta: Escaldar, pelar y cortar el tomate en daditos. Infusionar el romero en el aceite. Emulsionar el zumo del limón con el aceite de romero una vez frío. Finalmente mezclar con los daditos de tomate.

1 lb of monkfish
12 green asparagus
8 spring onions
1 lemon
100 ml of olive oil
1 ripe tomato
2 twigs of rosemary

Caramelize the spring onions in olive oil and sear the asparagus. Set aside.
Cut the monkfish in small pieces and grill.

Grill the asparagus and spring onions until ready. Set aside.
To serve: Place the hot monkfish over a layer of asparagus and spring onions and season with vinaigrette.
Vinaigrette: Peel, cut and dice the tomato. Heat the rosemary in oil. Mix the lemon juice and the rosemary oil once cool. Mix with the diced tomatos.

500 g Seeteufel
12 grüne Spargelstangen
8 Frühlingszwiebeln
1 Zitrone
100 ml Olivenöl
1 reife abgeschreckte, gepellte und in Würfel geschnittene Tomate
2 Rosmarinzweiglein

Die Frühlingszwiebeln in Olivenöl einmachen und den Spargel blanchieren. Beiseite stellen.
Den Seeteufel in kleine Stücke schneiden und auf der heißen Metallplatte nach Geschmack braten.
Spargel und Frühlingszwiebeln auf der Metallplatte anbraten. Beiseite stellen.
Serviervorschlag: Die heißen Seeteufelstückchen auf ein Bett aus Spargel und Frühlingszwiebeln legen und mit der Vinaigrette begießen.
Vinaigrette: Die Tomate abschrecken, pellen und in Würfel schneiden. Den Rosmarin in heißem Öl einlegen. Den Zitronensaft mit dem abgekühlten Rosmarinöl verrühren. Am Ende die Tomatenwürfel dazugeben.

500 g de lotte
12 asperges vertes
8 oignons tendres
1 citron
100 ml d'huile d'olive
1 tomate mûre
2 branches de romarin

Faire confire les oignons tendres dans l'huile d'olive et échauder les asperges. Réserver.
Couper la lotte en petits morceaux pour la braiser jusqu'au point de cuisson souhaité.
Braiser les asperges et les oignons tendres pour simplement les marquer. Réserver.
Présentation : Disposer la lotte bien chaude sur un lit d'asperges et d'oignons tendres et assaisonner de vinaigrette.
Vinaigrette : Échauder, peler et couper le tomate. Infuser le romarin dans l'huile. Réaliser une émulsion avec le jus du citron et l'huile au romarin refroidie. Mélanger enfin avec les dés de tomate.

500 g di coda di rospo
12 asparagi verdi (12 unità)
8 cipollotti
1 limone
100 ml di olio d'oliva
1 pomodoro maturo
2 rametti di rosmarino

Dorare i cipollotti in olio d'oliva e sbollentare gli asparagi. Mettere da parte.
Tagliare la coda di rospo a piccoli pezzi e passarli sulla griglia fino al punto di cottura desiderato.
Passare un momento gli asparagi e i cipollotti sulla griglia. Riservare.
Presentazione: Collocare la coda di rospo ben calda su un letto di asparagi e cipollotti e condire con la vinagrette.
Vinagrette: Sbollire, pelare e tagliare a dadino il pomodoro. Aromatizzare l'olio col rosmarino. Sbattere il limone con l'olio al rosmarino quando si è raffreddato. Alla fine mescolare con i dadini di pomodoro.

Pucca

Design: Fernando Sancheschulz | Chef: David Arguello

Passeig Picasso 32 | 08003 Barcelona
Phone: +34 932 687 236
pucca@wanadoo.es
Subway: Arc de Triomf, Barceloneta
Opening hours: Winter Tue–Sat 9 am to 2 am, summer Tue–Sat 1:30 pm to 2 am
Average price: € 30
Cuisine: Mexasian (Mexican and Asian fusion)
Special features: Very trendy

Pulpo marinado
en axiote

Octopus Marinated in Annatto

Oktopus in Axiote-Marinade

Poulpe mariné en axiote

Polpo marinato in pasta di semi di axiote

1 pulpo mediano
2 kg de boniatos
100 g de mantequilla
1 l de zumo de naranja natural
3 cucharadas de vinagre blanco
100 g de pasta de axiote
Sal y pimienta fresca

Congelar el pulpo durante al menos 24 horas y descongelar en el frigorífico. Poner abundante agua con sal a hervir y sumergir el pulpo cuando llegue al punto de ebullición durante 10 segundos, siempre empleando un instrumento de madera. Esperar a que el agua vuelva a hervir y repetir la operación. Así hasta tres veces. La cuarta vez el pulpo se deja hirviendo duran-te 20 minutos por cada kilo que pesa. Dejar enfriar en la misma agua.

Se prepara un adobo con la pasta de axiote, el zumo de naranja, el vinagre, la sal y la pimienta y se marinan las patas del pulpo enteras duran-te unas 12 horas.

Puré de boniato: Se envuelven los boniatos en papel de plata y se meten en el horno a 180 °C unos 20 minutos. Una vez cocidos se trituran con un tenedor agregando sal, pimienta y man-tequilla.

Emplatado: Calentar una pata en un sartén a fuego fuerte con un poco de aceite. Se monta sobre una base de puré de boniato y se adorna con julianas finas de puerro fritas.

1 medium-sized octopus
4 1/2 lb of sweet potato
3 1/2 oz of butter
1 l of freshly squeezed orange juice
3 tbsp of white vinegar
3 1/2 oz annatto paste
Salt and freshly ground pepper

Freeze the octopus for at least 24 hours and de-freeze in the refrigerator. Place the octopus in boiling water with salt for 10 seconds, using a wooden utensil. Wait until the water begins to boil again and repeat three times. The fourth time, leave the octopus to boil for 10 minutes per pound of weight. Let cool in the same water.

Prepare a marinade with the annatto paste, or-ange juice, vinegar, salt and pepper to marinate the octopus legs for 12 hours.

Sweet potato puré: Wrap the sweet potatos in aluminium foil and place in the oven for 20 min-utes at 350 °F. Once ready, mash with a fork adding salt, pepper and butter.

To serve: Heat one octopus leg in a bit of oil on high fire. Place over a bed of sweet potato mash and adorn with slices of fried leek.

1 mittelgroßer Oktopus
2 kg Süßkartoffeln
100 g Butter
1 l frischgepresster Apfelsinensaft
3 EL weißer Essig
100 g Axiotepaste (Orleanstrauchfrucht)
Salz, frischgemahlener Pfeffer

Den Oktopus mindestens 24 Stunden einfrieren und im Kühlschrank wieder auftauen lassen. Reichlich Salzwasser zum Kochen bringen. Sobald es sprudelt, den Oktopus 10 Sekunden lang eintauchen (einen Holzlöffel benutzen). Warten, bis das Wasser wieder sprudelt und den Vorgang wiederholen. Dann noch ein drittes Mal eintauchen. Beim vierten Mal den Oktopus 20 Minuten je Kilo Gewicht kochen lassen. Im Kochwasser abkühlen lassen.
Eine Marinade aus Axiotepaste, Apfelsinensaft, Essig, Salz und Pfeffer zubereiten und die Oktopusarme 12 Stunden darin einlegen.
Süßkartoffelpüree: Die Süßkartoffeln in Alufolie einwickeln und bei 180 °C im Ofen backen. Sobald sie gar sind, mit einer Gabel zerquetschen und mit Salz, Pfeffer und Butter vermengen.
Serviervorschlag: Einen Oktopusarm in der Pfanne bei großer Hitze in ein wenig Öl erhitzen, auf ein Häufchen Süßkartoffelpüree legen und mit frittierten Lauchstreifen garnieren.

1 poulpe de taille moyenne
2 kg de patates douces
100 g de beurre
1 l de jus d'orange naturel
3 c. à soupe de vinaigre blanc
100 g de pâte d'axiote
Sel et poivre frais

Congeler le poulpe durant au moins 24 heures et le décongeler au réfrigérateur. Faire bouillir de l'eau en abondance, saler et immerger le poulpe au point d'ébullition durant 10 secondes, en utilisant toujours un ustensile en bois. Attendre le retour de l'ébullition et recommencer. Réaliser l'opération à trois reprises. À la quatrième reprise, laisser bouillir le poulpe (20 minutes pour chaque kilo de chair). Laisser refroidir sans changer l'eau.
Préparer une marinade avec la pâte d'axiote, le jus d'orange, le vinaigre, le sel et le poivre pour laisser mariner les pattes du poulpe – entières – pendant 12 heures.
Purée de patates douces : Envelopper les patates douces dans du papier aluminium et passer au four à 180 °C pendant 20 minutes. Une fois cuites, les écraser à la fourchette en ajoutant sel, poivre et beurre.
Présentation : Chauffer une patate à la poêle en poussant les feux, dans un peu d'huile. Monter sur une base de purée de patate douce et décorer d'une fine julienne de poireaux frits.

1 polpo medio
2 kg di patate dolci
100 g di burro
1 l di succo d'arancia
3 cucchiai di aceto bianco
100 g di pasta di axiote
Sale e pepe fresco

Congelare il polpo durante almeno 24 ore e scongelarlo nel frigorifero. Bollire abbondante acqua salata e gettare il polpo quando comincia il bollore, cuocendo 10 secondi e usando un utensile di legno per rimuoverlo. Aspettare che l'acqua torni a bollire e ripetere. Fare quest'operazione tre volte. La quarta volta si lascia bollire il polpo 20 minuti per ogni kilo di peso. Lasciarlo raffreddare nell'acqua di cottura.
Preparare una marinata con la pasta di axiote, il succo d'arancia, l'aceto, il sale e il pepe. Lasciar marinare i tentacoli del polpo interi durante 12 ore.
Purè di patate dolci: Si avvolgono le patate in alluminio e si mettono nel forno a 180 °C per 20 minuti circa. Quando sono cotte si tritano con una forchetta aggiungendo sale, pepe e burro.
Presentazione: Scaldare un tentacolo del polpo in padella con olio ad alta temperatura. Si dispone su una base di purè di patate dolci e si decora con una julienne di porri fritti.

El Raco d'en Freixa

Design: Francesc Rifé | Chef: Ramon Freixa

Carrer de Sant Elies 22 | 08006 Barcelona
Phone: +34 932 097 559
www.elracodenfreixa.com
Subway: Plaça Molina
Opening hours: Everyday 1 am to 3:30 pm
Average price: € 70 – € 80
Cuisine: Creative catalan
Special features: Honoured with a Michelin star, houses a cooking school

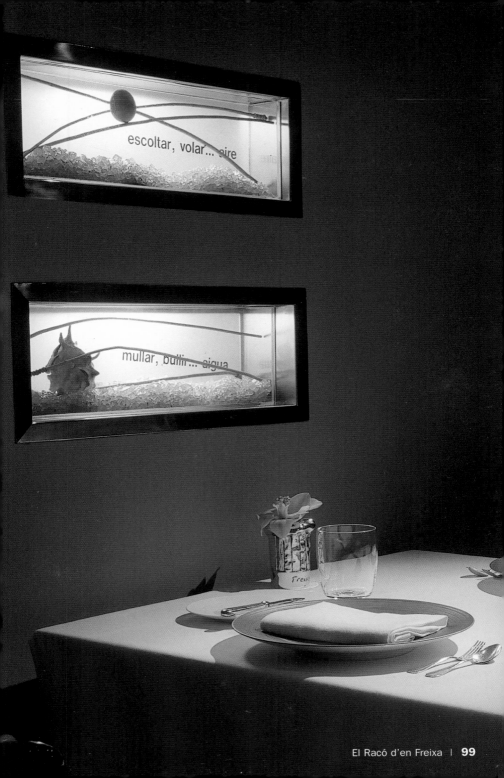

escoltar, volar... aire

mullar, bullir... aigua

Alcachofas

confitadas

Caramelized Artichokes

Eingemachte Artischocken

Artichauts confits

Carciofi sciroppati

Alcachofas confitadas:
1 l de aceite de oliva
2 kg de alcachofa de Benicarló
Aceite y sal
Laurel y pimienta de Jamaica

Limpiar las alcachofas, tornear y envasar al vacío con aceite de oliva, laurel y pimienta de Jamaica. Cocerlas al baño maría durante 3 horas a 60 °C. Enfriar y reservar hasta el momento de servir.

Crema de alcachofas con anisados:
2 kg de alcachofas
200 ml crema de leche
100 ml de aceite

500 ml de agua
Polvo de anisados
Yema de huevo
Estragón

Limpiar las alcachofas y saltearlas con aceite. Una vez doradas y escurridas, se cuecen en agua junto con la crema de leche, seguidamente, se trituran y se cuelan. Rectificar de sal y perfumar con el polvo de anisados.

Emplatado: Disponer en un plato una base de crema de alcachofas y sobre ella las alcachofas confitadas. Después se añade una yema de huevo y estragón, y se decora con chips de alcachofa.

Caramelized artichokes:
1 l of olive oil
4 1/2 lb of artichoke
Oil and salt
Bay leaves and Jamaican pepper

Wash, peel and place the artichoke in an airtight container with olive oil, bay leaves and Jamaican pepper. Double-boil for 4 hours at 140 °F. Cool down and refrigerate until ready to serve.

Aniseed-flavored cream of artichoke:
4 1/2 lb of artichoke
200 ml of cooking cream
100 ml of oil

500 ml of water
Aniseed powder
Egg yolk
Tarragon

Wash the artichokes and sauté in oil. Once golden and drained, cook in water together with the cream and once ready crush and strain. Add salt if needed and sprinkle with aniseed powder.

To serve: Pour a base of creme of artichoke on a plate, and place over it the crystallized artichoke. Then, add an egg yolk and tarragon and adorn with artichoke chips.

Eingemachte Artischocken:
1 l Olivenöl
2 kg Artischocken aus Benicarló
Öl und Salz
Lorbeer und Jamaicapfeffer

Die Artischocken säubern, rund schneiden und mit Lorbeer und Jamaicapfeffer ohne Lufteinschluss in Öl einlegen. Drei Stunden lang bei 60 °C im Wasserbad erhitzen. Abkühlen lassen und bis zum Servieren aufheben.

Artischockencreme mit Anis:
2 kg Artischocken
200 ml Sahne
100 ml Öl

500 ml Wasser
Anispulver
Eigelb
Estragon

Artischocken putzen, im Öl bräunen und abtropfen lassen. Dann mit Sahne im Wasser kochen, mit dem Mixstab zerkleinern und durch ein Sieb streichen. Mit Salz abschmecken und mit Anis würzen.

Serviervorschlag: Artischockencreme auf einem Teller ausbreiten und die eingemachten Artischocken darauf anordnen. Dann ein mit Estragon gewürztes Eigelb dazugeben und alles mit Artischockenchips garnieren.

Artichauts confits :
1 l d'huile d'olive
2 kg d'artichauts de Benicarló
Huile et sel
Laurier et piment de la Jamaique

Laver les artichauts, les nettoyer et les placer sous vide avec l'huile d'olive, du laurier et du piment de la Jamaïque. Les cuire au bain-marie durant 3 heures à 60 °C. Laisser refroidir et réserver jusqu'au service.

Crème d'artichauts anisée :
2 kg d'artichauts
200 ml de crème liquide
100 ml d'huile

500 ml d'eau
Graine d'anis en poudre
Jaune d'œuf
Estragon

Laver les artichauts et les faire sauter dans l'huile. Une fois dorés et égouttés, faire cuire dans l'eau avec la crème liquide pour ensuite les triturer et les égoutter. Assaisonner de sel et parfumer de graines d'anis en poudre.

Présentation : Disposer dans un plat une base de crème d'artichauts et la couvrir des artichauts confits. Ensuite, ajouter un jaune d'œuf et estragon, et décoré d'une feuille d'artichaut.

Carciofi sciroppati:
1 l di olio d'oliva
2 kg di carciofi di Benicarló
Olio e sale
Alloro e pepe della Giamaica

Pulire i carciofi, tornirli e imbottigliarli sotto vuoto con olio d'oliva, alloro e pepe della Giamaica. Cuocerli a bagno maria per 3 ore a 60 °C. Lasciar raffreddare e metterli da parte fino al momento di servire.

Crema di carciofi con anice:
2 kg di carciofi
200 ml di crema di latte

100 ml d'olio
500 ml d'acqua
Polvere d'anice
Tuorlo d'uovo
Dragoncello

Pulire i carciofi e rosolarli nell'olio. Quando sono dorati, sgocciolarli e cuocerli in acqua con la crema di latte, quindi tritarli e scolarli. Aggiustare il sale e profumare con polvere d'anice.

Presentazione: Disporre in un piatto una base di crema di carciofi e sopra i carciofi sciroppati. Alla fine aggiungere un tuorlo d'uovo e dragoncello, e decorare con chips di carciofi.

Salero

Design: Elsa Serra, Elena López, Pilar Líbano | Chef: Frank

Carrer del Rec 60 | 08003 Barcelona
Phone: +34 933 198 022
Subway: Arc de Triomf, Barceloneta
Opening hours: Mon–Thu 1:30 pm to 4 pm, and 9 pm to midnight,
Fri–Sat 9 pm to 1 am
Average price: € 21 – € 24
Cuisine: International
Special features: Very trendy, drinks, cocktails and music after dinner

Ensalada
de espinacas y pera

Spinach and Pear Salad

Salat aus Spinat und Birnen

Salade d'épinards et de poires

Insalata di spinaci e pera

Hojas de espinaca cruda
Brotes de alfalfa
1 alcachofa
1 pera
Pipas de calabaza
Pipas de girasol
Vinagreta con lima, miel y tomillo
Sal y pimienta

Lavar bien las espinacas con abundante agua, escurrir y reservar. Limpiar las alcachofas hasta obtener el corazón. Laminarlas finamente y saltearlas en una sartén con un poco de sal y pimienta.

Cortar la pera longitudinalmente y pasarla por la sartén con sal y pimienta hasta que adquiera un poco de color.
Vinagreta: Exprimir una lima, un poco de tomillo en polvo, miel, sal y aceite.
Emplatado: Disponer una base con las hojas de la espinaca, y agregar sobre ella las alcachofas y las peras. Decorar con alfalfa, y pipas de calabaza y de girasol. Finalmente, justo antes de servir, aliñar con la vinagreta.

Raw spinach leaves
Alfalfa sprouts
1 artichoke
1 pear
Pumpkin seeds
Sunflower seeds
Lime, honey and thyme vinagrette
Salt and pepper

Wash spinach, strain and set aside. Peel the artichoke to obtain the heart. Finely slice and sauté with a bit of salt and pepper.

Slice the pear longitudinally and sauté with salt and pepper until golden.
Vinaigrette: The juice of one lime, thyme powder, honey, salt and oil.
To serve: Lay the artichoke and pear over a base of spinach. Adorn with alfalfa sprouts, sunflower and pumpkin seeds. Just before serving, season with the vinaigrette.

Rohe Spinatblätter
Schneckenkleekeimlinge (Alfalfa)
1 Artischocke
1 Birne
Kürbiskerne
Sonnenblumenkerne
Vinaigrette aus Limone, Honig und Thymian
Salz und Pfeffer

Den Spinat gut abwaschen, abtropfen lassen und beiseite stellen. Die Artischocken putzen, bis nur das Herz übrigbleibt. In feine Scheibchen schneiden und in der Pfanne mit etwas Salz und Pfeffer sautieren.

Die Birne der Länge nach aufschneiden und mit Salz und Pfeffer in der Pfanne bräunen.
Vinaigrette: Eine Limone auspressen, den Saft mit Thymianpulver, Honig, Salz und Öl verrühren.
Serviervorschlag: Zuerst die Spinatblätter vorlegen, dann die Artischocken und Birnen darauf anordnen. Mit Schneckenkleekeimlingen und Kürbis- und Sonnenblumenkernen garnieren. Erst kurz vor dem Servieren die Vinaigrette darübergeben.

Feuilles d'épinards crues
Pousses d'alfalfa
1 artichaut
1 poire
Pépins de citrouille
Graines de tournesol
Vinaigrette au citron vert, miel et thym
Sel et Poivre

Bien laver les épinards avec de l'eau abondante, égoutter et réserver. Nettoyer les artichauts pour laisser uniquement le cœur. Les émincer assez finement puis les faire sauter à la poêle avec un peu de sel et de poivre.

Couper la poire dans le sens de la longueur et la passer à la poêle avec sel et poivre pour la colorer légèrement.
Vinaigrette : Presser un citron vert et mélanger avec un peu de thym en poudre, du miel, du sel et de l'huile.
Présentation : Disposer une base avec les feuilles d'épinards et couvrir avec les artichauts et les poires. Décorer de pousses d'alfalfa, de pépins de citrouille et de graines de tournesol. Enfin, juste avant de servir, assaisonner de vinaigrette.

Foglie crude di spinaci
Germogli di alfa alfa
1 carciofo
1 pera
Semi di zucca
Semi di girasole
Vinagrette di lime, miele e timo
Sale e pepe

Lavare bene gli spinaci, scolarli e metterli da parte. Pulire i carciofi mantenendo solo i cuori. Tagliarli a lamelle sottili e saltarli in padella con un po' di sale e pepe.

Tagliare la pera in senso longitudinale e passarla in padella con sale e pepe finchè prende un po' di colore.
Vinagrette: Spremere un lime, aggiungere un po' di timo in polvere, miele, sale e olio.
Presentazione: Fare una base di spinaci e aggiungere sopra i carciofi e le pere. Decorare con germogli di alfa alfa e semi di zucca e di girasole. Alla fine, appena prima di servire, condire con la vinagrette.

Santa Maria

Design: Alfons Tost | Chef: Paco Guzmán

Carrer Comerç 17 | 08003 Barcelona
Phone: +34 933 151 227
www.santamaria.biz
Subway: Jaume I, Arc de Triomf
Opening hours: Everyday 1:30 pm to 3:30 pm, and 8:30 pm to midnight
Average price: Tapas € 4 – € 12
Cuisine: Eclectic
Special features: Big window to the kitchen allows the clientelle to see the cooks

Ancas de rana
para Mireya

Frog Legs for Mireya

Froschschenkel für Mireya

Cuisses de grenouille pour Mireya

Cosce di rana per Mireya

1 kg de ancas de rana medianas
500 ml de salsa de soja
200 g de jengibre rallado
1 cucharada grande de miel
200 ml de aceite de girasol
1 cucharada de sésamo y cebollino
2 dientes de ajo picado

Para marinar las ancas de rana es necesario preparar una mezcla con soja, miel, dos dientes de ajo y jengibre rallado. Dejar reposar durante cuatro horas.
Transcurrido este tiempo, extraer las ancas de la marinada, ponerlas en un recipiente y guardarlas cuatro horas más en la nevera.
Después se escurren y se fríen en abundante aceite de girasol. Decorar con cebollino cortado en trocitos.

2 lb of medium-sized frog legs
500 ml of soy sauce
7 oz of grated ginger
1 large tbsp of honey
200 ml of sunflower oil
1 tbsp of sesame and chives
2 chopped cloves of garlic

Marinate the frog legs with a mix of soy sauce, honey, two cloves of garlic and grated ginger. Leave for four hours.
Remove the frog legs from the marinade and place inside a container for another four hours inside the refrigerator.
Drain and fry in abundant sunflower oil. Adorn with chopped chives.

1 kg mittelgroße Froschschenkel
500 ml Sojasoße
200 g geriebener Ingwer
1 großer EL Honig
200 ml Sonnenblumenöl
1 EL Sesamkörner und Schnittlauch
2 gehackte Knoblauchzehen

Um die Froschschenkel zu marinieren, wird eine Mischung aus Sojasoße, Honig, zwei Knoblauchzehen und geriebenem Ingwer zubereitet. Vier Stunden ziehen lassen.
Dann die Froschschenkel herausnehmen und vier Stunden in den Kühlschrank stellen.
Danach abtropfen lassen und in reichlich Sonnenblumenöl braten. Mit gehacktem Schnittlauch garnieren.

1 kg de cuisses de grenouille moyennes
500 ml sauce au soja
200 g de gingembre râpé
1 grosse c. à soupe de miel
200 ml d'huile de tournesol
1 c. à soupe de sésame et de ciboulette
2 pointes d'ail haché

Pour la marinade des cuisses de grenouille, préparer un mélange de soja, miel, deux pointes d'ail et de gingembre râpé. Laisser reposer quatre heures.
Le délai écoulé, extraire les cuisses de la marinade, les placer dans un récipient et les réserver quatre heures de plus au réfrigérateur.
Les égoutter ensuite pour les frire dans l'huile de tournesol. Décorer avec la ciboulette émincée.

1 kg di cosce di rana medie
500 ml di salsa di soia
200 g di zenzero grattugiato
1 cucchiaio grande di miele
200 ml di olio di girasole
1 cucchiaio di sesamo ed erba cipollina
2 denti d'aglio pestati

Per marinare le cosce di rana è necessario preparare una miscela con soia, miele, due denti d'aglio e zenzero grattugiato. Lasciar riposare quattro ore.
Trascorso questo tempo, estrarre le cosce dalla marinata, metterle in un recipiente e tenerle in frigo quattro ore.
Quindi si sgocciolano e si friggono in abbondante olio di girasole. Decorare con erba cipollina tagliata a pezzetti.

Saüc

Design: Laia Doñate I Chef: Xavier Franco

Passatge Lluís Pellicer 12 I 08036 Barcelona
Phone: +34 933 210 189
www.saucrestaurant.com
Subway: Hospital Clínic, Diagonal
Opening hours: Mon–Sat 1:30 pm to 3:30 pm, and 8:30 pm to 10:30 pm
Average price: € 45 – € 50
Cuisine: Creative Catalan
Special features: Refined ambience in a paradigmatic city alley

Papada
con calamares y alcachofas

Dewlap with Squid and Artichoke

Schweinewamme mit Tintenfischen und
Artischocken

Gorge de porc aux calmars et aux
artichauts

Sottomento di maiale con calamari e
carciofi

Papada: 500 g de papada de cerdo, 40 g de mantequilla, 1 l de caldo de ternera, tomillo, sal gorda, azúcar, pimentón y pimienta
Jugo de asado: 1 carcasa de pollo, 1 cebolla mediana, 2 tomates maduros, 5 granos de pimienta negra, 100 g de puerro, brandy
8 alcachofas medianas, 400 g de calamares, rúcula, perejil, cebollino, albahaca

Mezclar la sal gorda, el azúcar, la pimienta molida y el pimentón y cubrir la papada con la mezcla durante 4 horas. Lavar la papada y secar. En un cazo colocar los demás ingredientes y la papada y cocer con tapa a fuego muy lento 5 horas. Extraer la papada y refrigerarla hasta que endurezca. Cortarla en 4 lonchas y dorarla en una sartén a fuego suave y sin aceite.
Para el jugo de asado, cortar la carcasa en trozos. Ponerla en una cazuela con aceite y dorarla con los ajos, añadir la cebolla y el puerro cortados a láminas, el tomillo y los granos de pimienta. Reducir la intensidad del fuego para rehogar las verduras. Cuando adquieran un tono levemente dorado, agregar los tomates y rehogar durante 5 minutos. Mojar con un chorro de brandy y reducir hasta casi su total evaporación. Añadir 1 litro de agua y cocer muy lentamente con tapa durante 3 horas. Enfriar sin colar; una vez colado reducir el caldo resultante hasta que obtener una consistencia de salsa ligera. Salpimentar y reservar.
Confitar el corazón de las alcachofas en aceite de oliva hasta que estén tierna, dorar ligeramente en una sartén con aceite y mantequilla.
Pasar por la batidora las hierbas frescas con aceite de oliva para aliñar el plato.
Limpiar y hacer los calamares a la plancha.
Emplatar y decorar con la rúcula.

Dewlap: 1 lb of pork dewlap, 1 1/2 oz of butter, 1 qt of veal stock, thyme, rock salt, sugar, paprika and pepper
Baking sauce: 1 chicken skeleton, 1 medium-sized onion, 2 ripe tomatoes, 5 peppercorns, 3 1/2 oz of leek, brandy
8 medium-sized artichokes, 14 oz of squid, rocket salad, parsley, chives and basil

Cover the dewlap with a mix of rock salt, sugar, ground pepper and paprika and leave for 4 hours. Wash the dewlap and dry. In a pot, introduce the remaining ingredients and cover to cook on low fire for 5 hours. Take out the dewlap and refrigerate until hardened. Cut four slices and sauté on low heat, without oil, until golden.
For the sauce, chop the skeleton and sauté in oil with the garlic until golden, adding the onion, sliced leek, thyme and peppercorns. Lower the heat to sauté the vegetables. Once slightly golden, add the tomatoes and sauté for 5 minutes. Pour a bit of brandy and reduce until completely evaporated. Add 1 quart of water and cook on low heat for 3 hours, covering the pot. Strain once cold, reducing the stock to obtain the consistency of a light sauce. Add salt and pepper and set aside.
Crystallize the artichoke heart in olive until tender, and sauté in a pan with oil and butter until golden.
Pass the fresh herbs and olive oil through the blender to season.
Grill the squid, serve and adorn with rocket salad.

Fleisch: 500 g Schweinewamme, 40 g Butter, 1 l Kalbsbrühe, Thymian, grobkörniges Salz, Zucker, Paprika, Pfeffer
Bratensaft: 1 Hühnergerippe, 1 mittelgroße Zwiebel, 2 reife Tomaten, 5 schwarze Pfefferkörner, 100 g Lauch, Brandy
8 mittelgroße Artischocken, 400 g Tintenfische (Kalmare), Ruccola, Petersilie, Schnittlauch, Basilikum

Das grobkörnige Salz mit Zucker, Pfeffer und Paprika mischen, Wamme darin wenden und Mischung 4 Stunden lang ziehen lassen. Das Fleisch waschen und trocknen. Die restlichen Zutaten mit der Wamme in einen Topf geben und zugedeckt auf sehr kleiner Flamme 5 Stunden schmoren. Dann das Fleisch herausnehmen und abkühlen lassen, bis es fest wird. In 4 Scheiben schneiden und in der Pfanne bei schwacher Hitze ohne Öl bräunen.

Für den Bratensaft das Hühnergerippe in Stücke schneiden, mit Öl und Knoblauch in einem Topf anbraten, Zwiebel und Lauch in Ringe schneiden und zugeben, ebenso Thymian und Pfefferkörner. Um das Gemüse anzubraten, Hitze drosseln. Sobald es goldbraun ist, die Tomaten hineintun und noch fünf Minuten schmoren lassen. Einen Schuss Brandy dazugeben und die Flüssigkeit fast völlig verdampfen lassen. 1 l Wasser hinzugeben und zugedeckt 3 Stunden kochen lassen. Nach dem Abkühlen abseien. Die Flüssigkeit verdampfen lassen, bis eine leichte Soße entsteht, mit Salz und Pfeffer abschmecken. Die Artischockenherzen in Olivenöl einlegen, bis sie weich sind. In der Pfanne in Butter und Olivenöl leicht anbräunen.
Die frischen Kräuter mit dem Olivenöl verquirlen und zum Anmachen verwenden.
Tintenfische putzen und auf heißer Platte braten. Mit Ruccola garnieren und servieren.

Gorge : 500 g de gorge de porc, 40 g de beurre, 1 l de bouillon de veau, thym, gros sel, sucre, paprika et poivre
Jus de rôti : 1 carcasse de poulet, 1 oignon moyen, 2 tomates mûres, 5 grains de poivre noir, 100 g de poireaux, l'eau-de-vie
8 artichauts moyens, 400 g de calmars, roquette, persil, ciboulette, basilic

Mélanger le gros sel, le sucre, le poivre moulu et le paprika et en recouvrir la gorge pendant 4 heures. Laver la gorge et la sécher. Dans une casserole, disposer les autres ingrédients et la gorge puis laisser cuire à couvert, à feu doux, pendant 5 heures. Extraire la gorge et la refroidir pour la faire durcir. La couper en 4 tranches et la dorer à la poêle à feu doux, sans huile.
Pour le jus de rôti, couper la carcasse en morceaux. Les passer à la casserole avec l'huile et faire dorer avec l'ail, en ajoutant ensuite l'oignon et le poireau émincés, le thym et les grains de piment. Réduire le feu pour frire à feu doux les légumes. Lorsqu'ils prennent une teinte légèrement dorée, ajouter les tomates et frire durant 5 minutes. Mouiller avec un trait d'eau-de-vie et faire réduire jusqu'à évaporation totale. Ajouter 1 litre d'eau et cuire très lentement à couvert pendant 3 heures. Laisser refroidir sans égoutter. Une fois égoutté, réduire le bouillon obtenu jusqu'à qu'il prenne une consistance de sauce légère. Saler, poivrer et réserver.
Faire confire les cœurs d'artichaut dans l'huile d'olive pour les rendre tendres. Puis faire dorer légèrement à la poêle avec huile et beurre. Passer au mixer les herbes fraîches avec l'huile d'olive pour assaisonner le plat.
Nettoyer les calmars pour les préparer au grill. Disposer dans le plat et décorer avec la roquette.

Sottomento: 500 g di sottomento di maiale, 40 g di burro, 1 l di brodo di manzo, timo, sale grosso, zucchero, paprica e pepe
Sugo dell'arrosto: 1 carcassa di pollo, 1 cipolla media, 2 pomodori maturi, 5 grani di pepe nero, 100 g di porro, brandy
8 carciofi mediani, 400 g di calamari, rucola, prezzemolo, erba cipollina, basilico

Mescolare il sale grosso, lo zucchero, il pepe macinato e la paprica e coprire il sottomento con l'impasto lasciandolo riposare 4 ore. Lavare la carne e asciugarla. Mettere in un tegame gli ingredienti rimasti e il sottomento e cuocere, col coperchio, a fuoco basso per 5 ore. Estrarre il sottomento e refrigerarlo finché diventa duro. Tagliarlo in quattro tranci e dorarlo in padella a fuoco basso e senza olio.
Per il sugo dell'arrosto, tagliare la carcassa di pollo a pezzi. Metterla in una casseruola con olio e dorarla con l'aglio, aggiungere la cipolla e il porro tagliato a lamelle, il timo e i grani di pepe. Ridurre l'intensità del fuoco per rosolare le verdure. Quando prendono un tono leggermente dorato aggiungere i pomodori e rosolare 5 minuti. Bagnare con una spruzzata di brandy e ridurre fino a quasi totale evaporazione. Aggiungere 1 litro d'acqua e cuocere molto lentamente, coperto, durante 3 ore. Raffreddare. Dopo averlo filtrato ridurre il brodo restante fino alla consistenza di una salsa leggera. Salare e mettere da parte.
Cuocere i cuori di carciofo in olio d'oliva finché diventano teneri, dorare leggermente in padella con olio e burro.
Frullare le erbe fresche con olio d'oliva per condire il piatto. Pulire e passare sulla piastra i calamari. Servire sul piatto e decorare con la rucola.

Shibui

Design: José Bruguera | Chef: Ryu Myung Su

Carrer Comte d'Urgell 272 | 08036 Barcelona
Phone: +34 933 219 004
www.shibuirestaurantes.com
Subway: Hospital Clínic
Opening hours: Everyday 1 pm to 3:30 pm and 8:30 pm to 11:30 pm
Average price: € 24 – € 36
Cuisine: Japanese
Special features: Trendy, one of the best Japanese restaurants in town

Sushi no

moriawase

150 g de arroz
20 ml de vinagre de arroz
40 g de atún
40 g de salmón
40 g de breca
40 g de rodaballo
40 g de dentón
40 g de jurel
4 langostinos
1 cucharadita de azúcar
1 cucharadita de sal
4 laminas de alga nori
2 cucharadas de salsa de soja
15 g wasabi
15 g jengibre encurtido

Lavar el arroz, cocerlo al vapor y dejarlo en reposo un cuarto de hora aproximadamente. Ponerlo en un cuenco grande y mezclarlo con cuidado con el vinagre de arroz, el azúcar y la sal. Cortar en finas lonchas el atún, el salmón, la breca, el rodaballo, el dentón y el jurel. Escaldar los langostinos y cortarlos a lo largo.
Sushis: Formar bolas alargadas de arroz aderezado con un poco de wasabi en la parte superior y cubrirlas con las diferentes lonchas de pescado.
Makis: Se extiende una lamina de alga nori encima de una esterilla de bambú, luego un poco de arroz y una tira de pescado con un poco de wasabi; se enrolla presionando a lo largo del rollo. Después se corta en porciones de 2,5 cm aproximadamente.
Se colocan los sushis y los makis en una fuente y se sirve acompañado de jengibre encurtido, wasabi y un bol con salsa de soja.

5 oz of rice
20 ml of rice vinegar
1 1/2 oz of tuna
1 1/2 oz of salmon
1 1/2 oz red bream
1 1/2 oz of turbot
1 1/2 oz toothed bream
1 1/2 oz of horse mackerel
4 prawns
1 tsp of sugar
1 tsp of salt
4 sheets of nori seaweed
2 tbsp of soy sauce
1 tbsp of wasabi
1 tbsp pickled ginger

Wash the rice, steam and allow to settle for approximately 15 minutes. Place in a large bowl and mix carefully with the rice vinegar, sugar and salt. Finely slice the tuna, salmon, red beam, turbot, the toothed bream and the horse mackerel. Sear the prawns and cut lengthwise.
Sushis: Mold elongated balls of rice, season with a bit of wasabi on top and cover with different slices of fish.
Makis: Extend a sheet of nori seaweed over a bamboo mat and place rice and a strip of fish with a bit of wasabi; roll applying pressure along the length of the roll. Cut into approximately 1 in portions.
Place the sushis and makis in a platter and serve with pickled ginger, wasabi and a bowl with soy sauce.

150 g Reis
20 ml Reisessig
40 g Tunfisch
40 g Lachs
40 g kleine Rotbrasse
40 g Steinbutt
40 g Zahnbrasse
40 g Makrele
4 Langostinos
1 TL Zucker
1 TL Salz
4 Scheiben Nori-Algen
2 EL Sojasoße
15 g Wasabi (japanischer Meerrettich)
15 g eingelegter Ingwer

Den Reis waschen, im Dampf kochen und etwa eine Viertelstunde ruhen lassen. In eine große Schüssel füllen und behutsam mit Reisessig, Zucker und Salz vermischen.
Den Tunfisch, den Lachs, die Rotbrasse, den Steinbutt, die Makrele und die Zahnbrasse in dünne Scheiben schneiden. Die Langostinos abbrühen und der Länge nach aufschneiden.
Sushis: Aus dem Reis längliche Kugeln formen, oben mit etwas Wasabi würzen und mit Scheiben der verschiedenen Fischsorten bedecken.
Makis: Eine Scheibe Nori-Alge auf einer Bambusmatte ausbreiten, etwas Reis und einen Streifen Fisch mit etwas Wasabi dara" auflegen. Beim Aufrollen gleichmäßig über die ganze Länge drücken. In je etwa 2,5 cm lange Stückchen schneiden.
Sushis und Makis auf einen Präsentierteller legen und mit eingelegtem Ingwer, Wasabi und einem Schälchen Sojasoße servieren.

150 g de riz
20 ml de vinaigre de riz
40 g de thon
40 g de saumon
40 g de daurade
40 g de turbot
40 g de denté
40 g de chinchard
4 langoustines
1 c. à café de sucre
1 c. à café de sel
4 feuilles d'algue nori
2 c. à soupe de sauce soja
15 g de wasabi
15 g de gingembre au vinaigre

Laver le riz, le cuire à la vapeur et le laisser reposer un quart d'heure environ. Le placer dans une grande jatte et le mélanger avec soin au vinaigre de riz, au sucre et au sel.
Émincer finement le thon, le saumon, la daurade, le turbot, le chinchard et le denté. Échauder les langoustines et les couper en long.
Sushis : Former des boulettes allongées de riz assaisonné avec un peu de wasabi sur le dessus et les couvrir avec les tranches de poisson.
Makis : Étendre une feuille d'algue nori sur une paille de bambou, ajouter une peu de riz et une tranche de poisson avec un peu de wasabi. Enrouler en appuyant sur la longueur du rouleau. Couper ensuite des portions de 2,5 cm environ.
Disposer les sushis et les makis dans un plat et les servir accompagnés de gingembre au vinaigre, de wasabi et d'un bol de sauce soja.

150 g di riso
20 ml di aceto di riso
40 g di tonno
40 g di salmone
40 g di pagello
40 g di rombo
40 g di dentice
40 g di tracuro
4 gamberoni
1 cucchiaino di zucchero
1 cucchiaino di sale
4 lamine di alga nori
2 cucchiai di salsa di soia
15 g wasabi
15 g zenzero sottaceto

Lavare il riso, cuocerlo al vapore e lasciarlo riposare un quarto d'ora circa. Metterlo in una ciotola grande e mescolarlo con attenzione con l'aceto di riso, lo zucchero e il sale.
Tagliare a fette sottili il tonno, il salmone, il pagello, il rombo, il dentice e il tracuro. Sbollentare i gamberoni e tagliarli nel senso della lunghezza.
Sushi: Formare delle palline allungate di riso, insaporito con un poco di wasabi nella parte superiore, e coprirle con le diverse fette di pesce.
Makis: Stendere una lamina di alga nori su una piccola stuoia di bambù, quindi un poco di riso e una striscia di pesce con un po' di wasabi; si arrotola premendo lungo il rotolo. Poi si taglia in porzioni di 2,5 cm circa.
Collocare sushi e makis in un piatto da portata e servire accompagnato da zenzero sottaceto, wasabi e una ciotola di salsa di soia.

Phone: +34 933 644 517
www.tatibarcelona.com
Subway: Zona Universitària
Opening hours: Tue–Sat 9 pm to 3 am
Average price: € 55
Cuisine: Creative Mediterranean
Special features: Music after midnight, 50's style and decoration

Merluza gratinada
con erizos de mar

Hake au Gratin with Sea Urchin

Gratinierter Seehecht mit Seeigeln

Merlu gratiné aux oursins de mer

Merluzzo gratinato con ricci di mare

4 supremas de merluza de palangre de 170 g
160 g de calabaza
160 g de patata
8 dientes de ajo
40 g de yemas de erizo
80 ml de nata líquida
Aceite de oliva
Sal y pimienta

Puré de calabaza: Cocer la calabaza y pasarla por la batidora añadiendo el agua de su cocción hasta obtener el espesor de una salsa. Agregar un chorrito de aceite de oliva y salpimentar.

Puré de patata violeta: Cocer la patata y pasarla por la batidora junto con los dientes de ajo previamente dorados. Añadir el agua de su cocción hasta obtener el espesor de una salsa. Agregar un chorrito de aceite de oliva y salpimentar.
Gratinado de erizo: Reducir la nata líquida, retirarla del fuego y añadir las yemas de erizo. Triturar.
Dorar a la sartén las supremas de merluza salpimentadas.
Emplatado: Preparar un lecho con el puré de calabaza y el de patata y disponer la merluza. Cubrir con la crema de erizo y gratinar.

4 filets of hake (6 oz each)
5 1/2 oz of pumpkin
5 1/2 oz of potato
8 cloves of garlic
1 1/2 oz of sea urchin roe
80 ml of cream
Olive oil
Salt and pepper

Pumpkin purée: Boil the pumpkin and mix in the blender adding the water used to boil, until obtaining the thickness of a sauce. Drizzle with olive oil and add salt and pepper.

Violet potato purée: Boil the potatoes and mix in the blender with two cloves of garlic previously sautéed until golden. Add the water used to boil until obtaining the thickness of a sauce. Drizzle with olive oil and add salt and pepper.
Sea urchin gratin: Reduce the cream, remove from the heat and add the sea urchin roe. Blend.
Sauté the hake filets until golden, adding salt and pepper.
To serve: Prepare a bed of pumpkin and potato purée for the hake filets. Cover with sea urchin cream and cook au gratin.

4 etwa 170 g schwere frische Seehechtfilets
160 g Kürbis
160 g Kartoffeln
8 Knoblauchzehen
40 g Seeigel
80 ml Sahne
Olivenöl
Salz und Pfeffer

Kürbispüree: Den Kürbis kochen und mit dem Mixstab pürieren. Dabei so viel Kochwasser hinzufügen, bis die Konsistenz einer Soße entsteht. Einen Schuss Olivenöl dazugeben, mit Salz und Pfeffer abschmecken.

Püree aus roten Kartoffeln: Kartoffeln kochen und zusammen mit den zuvor angebratenen Knoblauchzehen pürieren. Kochwasser hinzufügen, bis die Konsistenz einer Soße entsteht. Einen Schuss Olivenöl dazugeben und mit Salz und Pfeffer abschmecken.

Seeigelcreme: Die Sahne erhitzen und durch Verdunsten eindicken, vom Feuer nehmen, das Seeigelfleisch dazugeben und mit dem Rührstab mixen.

Die gewürzten Seehechtfilets in der Pfanne bräunen.

Serviervorschlag: Ein Bett aus Kürbis- und Kartoffelpüree bereiten und den Seehecht darüberlegen. Mit Seeigelcreme begießen und überbacken.

---

4 suprêmes de merlu de palangre de 170 g
160 g de citrouille
160 g de pommes de terre
8 pointes d'ail
40 g de cœurs d'oursin
80 ml de crème liquide
Huile d'olive
Sel et poivre

Purée de citrouille : Cuire la citrouille et la passer au mixer en ajoutant de l'eau de cuisson pour obtenir l'épaisseur d'une sauce. Ajouter un trait d'huile d'olive, du sel et du poivre.

Purée de pomme de terre violette : Cuire les pommes de terre et la passer au mixer avec les pointes d'ail dorées auparavant. Ajouter l'eau de cuisson pour obtenir l'épaisseur d'une sauce. Ajouter un trait d'huile d'olive, du sel et du poivre.

Gratin d'oursin : Faire réduire la crème liquide, la retirer du feu et ajouter les cœurs d'oursin. Mélanger.

Faire dorer à la poêle les suprêmes de merlu salés et poivrés.

Présentation : Préparer un lit de purée de citrouille et de purée de pomme de terre et disposer le merlu. Couvrir de la crème d'oursin et faire gratiner.

---

4 supreme di merluzzo di palangaro da 170 g
160 g di zucca
160 g di patate
8 denti di aglio
40 g di polpa di ricci
80 ml di panna liquida
Olio d'oliva
Sale e pepe

Purè di zucca: Cuocere la zucca e frullarla aggiungendo l'acqua di cottura fino ad ottenere lo spessore di una salsa. Aggiungere una spruzzata d'olio d'oliva e salare.

Purè di patate color viola: Cuocere le patate e frullarle insieme ai denti d'aglio dopo averli dorati. Aggiungere l'acqua di cottura fino ad ottenere lo spessore di una salsa. Aggiungere una spruzzata d'olio e salare.

Ricci gratinati: Far ridurre la panna liquida, ritirarla dal fuoco e aggiungere la polpa dei ricci. Triturare.

Dorare in padella le supreme di merluzzo salate e pepate.

Presentazione: Preparare un fondo col purè di zucca e quello di patate e disporre il merluzzo. Coprire con la crema di ricci e gratinare.

Torre d'Alta Mar

Design: Cristina Rodríguez | Chef: Óscar Pérez

Passeig Joan de Borbó 88 | 08003 Barcelona
Phone: +34 932 210 007
www.torredealtamar.com
Subway: Barceloneta
Opening hours: Everyday 1 pm to 3:30 pm, and 8:45 pm to 11:30 pm
Average price: € 70 – € 80
Cuisine: Actualized Mediterranean Catalan
Special features: Spectacular views of the city

PIERRE OU PAUL

Atadillos
de bacalao y bogavante

Codfish and Lobster

Stockfischroulade mit Hummer

Paupiettes de morue et homard

Involtino di baccalà e astice

1 bogavante azul de 500 g
300 g morro de bacalao desalado y congelado
1 puerro confitado cortado a tiras
2 espárragos trigueros verdes
200 ml de aceite de oliva de 0,4°
Sal
Pimienta negra
Pimienta de Jamaica en grano
Cardamomo verde en grano
Vinagreta de cebolleta, tomate y cebollino
100 g de pasta fresca al gusto
20 g de orejones de tomate
20 g de mostaza Pommery

Separar la cabeza del bogavante y hervir el resto con agua y sal, pimienta de Jamaica y cardamomo durante unos 12 minutos. Enfriar, pelar y trinchar. Extraer el coral de la cabeza y saltear con un poco de aceite, sal y pimienta negra. Mezclar con el resto de la carne del bogavante. Con el resto de la cabeza, hacer un aceite de marisco simplemente dorando las cáscaras, cubriéndolas de aceite y dejando hervir durante 10 minutos. Posteriormente triturar y colar con malla fina.

Forrar un molde con el bacalao cortado con un cortafiambres. Rellenarlo con la masa de bogavante preparada, un poco de puerro confitado y los espárragos hervidos y cortados a trozos pequeños. Cerrar los moldes de manera que el bacalao lo envuelva todo.

Colocar el bogavante y bacalao al lado de la pasta hervida y fría. Aliñar con la vinagreta, la mostaza, los orejones de tomate picados y el aceite de marisco.

1 blue lobster (1 lb)
10 1/2 oz of desalted and frozen codfish snout
1 caramelized leek cut in strips
2 green asparagus
200 ml of olive oil 0,4°
Salt
Black pepper
Jamaican peppercorns
Green cardamom seeds
Spring onion, tomato and chives vinaigrette
3 1/2 oz of fresh pasta
1/2 oz of dried tomato
1/2 oz of Pommery mustard

Separate the lobster head and boil the rest in water with salt, Jamaican pepper and cardamom for 12 minutes. Cool down, peel and cut up. Extract the coral from the head and sauté in a bit of olive oil with salt and pepper. Mix with the remaining lobster meat. With the rest of the head, make a seafood oil by sautéing the shells, covering with oil and boiling for 10 minutes. Afterwards, mix in the blender and strain through a fine mesh.

Line a mold with finely sliced codfish and fill with the lobster meat, a bit of crystallized leek and boiled asparagus cut into small pieces. Cover the molds entirely with the codfish slices.

Put the lobster and codfish next to the boiled cooled pasta. Season with the vinaigrette, the mustard, chopped dried tomatos and the seafood oil.

1 blauer Hummer (500 g)
300 g entsalzener, tiefgefrorener Stockfisch
1 eingemachtes Lauch, in Streifen geschnitten
2 Stangen wilder grüner Spargel
200 ml Olivenöl (Säuregrad 0,4°)
Salz
Schwarzer Pfeffer
Jamaicapfefferkörner
Grüne Kardamomkörner
Vinaigrette aus Frühlingszwiebeln, Schnittlauch und Tomate
100 g frische Nudeln
20 g getrocknete Tomaten
20 g Pommerysenf

Den Kopf des Hummers abtrennen und den Rest in Wasser mit Salz, Jamaicapfeffer und Kardamom etwa zwölf Minuten kochen. Abkühlen lassen, das Fleisch herauslösen und zerquetschen. Die Reste aus dem Kopf nehmen, in etwas Öl sautieren und mit Salz und Pfeffer abschmecken. Mit dem Rest des Hummerfleisches vermischen. Aus dem Rest des Hummerkopfes ein Krustentieröl bereiten: Die Schalen anbraten, mit Öl bedecken und zehn Minuten im siedenden Öl ziehen lassen. Zerstoßen und durch ein feines Sieb gießen.
Kleine Formen mit dem in feine Scheiben geschnittenen Stockfisch auslegen und mit der Hummerfleischmasse sowie etwas eingelegtem Lauch und dem gekochten und in kleine Stücke geschnittenen Spargel auffüllen. Die Stockfischscheiben so einschlagen, dass alles bedeckt ist.
Das Hummerfleisch und den Stockfisch neben den gekochten abgekühlten Nudeln servieren. Die gekochten und abgekühlten Nudeln mit Vinaigrette, Senf, gehackten Trockentomaten und Krustentieröl anmachen.

1 homard bleu de 500 g
300 g de museau de morue dessalée et congelée
1 poireau confit en lanières
2 asperges vertes sauvages
200 ml d'huile d'olive (acidité 0,4°)
Sel
Poivre noir
Piment de la Jamaïque en grains
Cardamome verte en grains
Vinaigrette d'oignon tendre, tomate et ciboulette
100 g de pâtes fraîches, selon les goûts
20 g d'oreillons de tomate
20 g de moutarde de Pommery

Séparer la tête du homard et faire bouillir le reste dans de l'eau assaisonnée de sel, piment de la Jamaïque et cardamome durant 12 minutes. Laisser refroidir, peler et découper. Extraire le corail de la tête et faire sauter dans un peu d'huile, du sel et du poivre noir. Mélanger avec le reste de la chair du homard. Avec le reste de la tête, préparer une huile de crustacé simplement en faisant dorer les carapaces, en les couvrant d'huile et en laissant bouillir durant 10 minutes. Ensuite, écraser et passer au chinois à tamis fin.
Dresser un moule avec la morue coupée à la trancheuse. Le remplir avec la pâte de homard préparée, un peu de poireau confit et les asperges bouillies et découpées en petits morceaux. Fermer les moules de sorte que la morue enveloppe le tout.
Disposer la morue et l'homard a coté de la pâte bouillie et froide. Assaisonner avec la vinaigrette, la moutarde, les oreillons de tomate hachés et l'huile de crustace.

1 astice blu da 500 g
300 g di baccalà dissalato e congelato
1 porro sciroppato tagliato a strisce
2 asparagi verdi
200 ml di olio d'oliva di 0,4° di acidità
Sale
Pepe nero
Pepe di Giamaica in grani
Cardamomo verde in grani
Vinagrette di cipollotti, pomodori ed erba cipollina
100 g di pasta fresca a scelta
20 g di pomodori secchi
20 g di senape Pommery

Separare la testa dell'astice e bollire il resto in acqua e sale, pepe di Giamaica e cardamomo per circa 12 minuti. Raffreddare, pelare e tritare. Estrarre il corallo dalla testa e saltare con un poco d'olio, sale e pepe nero. Mescolare col resto della polpa dell'astice. Col resto della testa fare un olio i frutti di mare semplicemente dorando i gusci, coprendoli d'olio e lasciando bollire 10 minuti. Quindi tritare e filtrare con un colino a maglia fitta.
Foderare uno stampo col baccalà tagliato con un'affettatrice. Riempirlo con la polpa dell'astice preparata, un poco di porri sciroppati e gli asparagi bolliti e tagliati a piccoli pezzi. Chiudere lo stampo in modo che il baccalà lo copra del tutto.
Collocare il baccalà e il astice con la pasta bollita e raffreddata. Condire con la vinagrette, la senape, i pomodori secchi e l'olio di frutti di mare.

EIXAMPLE

16

onda de Sant Pere

Avinguda Meridiana

SANT MARTÍ

10
8
20
12   17
SC ANTIC

Parc de la
Ciutadella

2
19

1

BARCELONETA

3 7 4

Cool Restaurants

Size: 14 x 21.5 cm / 5 1/2 x 8 in.
136 pp
Flexicover
c. 130 color photographs
Text in English, German, French,
Spanish and (*) Italian

Other titles in the same series:

Amsterdam (*)
ISBN 3-8238-4588-8

Berlin (*)
ISBN 3-8238-4585-3

Hamburg (*)
ISBN 3-8238-4599-3

London
ISBN 3-8238-4568-3

Los Angeles (*)
ISBN 3-8238-4589-6

Milan (*)
ISBN 3-8238-4587-X

New York
ISBN 3-8238-4571-3

Paris
ISBN 3-8238-4570-5

Tokyo (*)
ISBN 3-8238-4590-X

To be published in the
same series:

Brussels	Munich
Chicago	Rome
Geneva	Stockholm
Madrid	Sydney
Miami	Vienna
Moscow	Zurich

teNeues